YOU'RE EITHER WALKING THE WALK OR JUST RUNNING YOUR MOUTH!

Verse-By-Verse Study Of The Book Of James

Todd Linn

Preaching Truth Publishing

PREACHING TRUTH

Praise for *You're Either Walking*

"This is a wonderful verse-by-verse study of the Book of James! It will serve as a valuable resource for the pastor who preaches through James or the teacher leading a small group Bible study. Dr. Linn outlines the passages and provides very helpful exegetical insights. I will certainly use this excellent work in my own preaching and teaching!"

—Daniel L. Akin
President, Southeastern Baptist Theological Seminary

"Practical, insightful, exegetically sound, and delightfully written, Todd Linn's exposition of James is a joy to read and makes me want to preach through this book all over again! I know of no other book that combines the clear and careful analysis of a scholar with the deft insights of a seasoned pastor like this one."

—Hershael H. York
Dean, The School of Theology
Professor of Preaching at Southern Seminary

To my wonderful wife Michele who, second only to Jesus, makes sure that I "walk the walk."

"If you would not be forgotten as soon as you are dead and rotten, either write things worth reading, or do things worth the writing."

--BENJAMIN FRANKLIN, POOR RICHARD'S ALMANACK

Contents

Preface

Welcome to the first edition of the Preaching Truth series! It is my hope that this series will be an affordable help to pastors, lay leaders, and any person interested in a straightforward verse-by-verse study of books of the Bible.

These chapters are largely the product of my weekly studies as I prepared each exposition for Sunday preaching. They have been modified to suit the present format, but largely retain their original form including the placing of the biblical text at the beginning of each exposition (New King James Version unless otherwise noted).

Prominent placement of the biblical text is a personal conviction. The life-changing power of Bible-study comes directly from the Word itself. This format also aids the reader by providing an easy way to refer back to the biblical text while reading through the chapters.

As something of a disclaimer I freely admit that, to quote the popular song lyric, "I get by with a little help from my friends." As I studied the Book of James during sermon preparation I frequently listened to or read sermons from some of my favorite expositors—Alistair Begg, Ligon Duncan, and Tim Keller, to name a few. Nearly every preacher is blessed by the studies of others.

As a matter of integrity, however, preachers must produce their own expositions. It has always been my practice to "milk a lot of cows, but churn my own butter." Not only is plagiarism wrong, but it robs the preacher of the joy of discovering truth for himself and sharing that truth in his own way as God guides.

Nevertheless we invariably make mistakes, sometimes forgetting where a particular statement or phrase originated. While I have taken care to credit sources, I have likely erred here and there and will speedily correct future editions where necessary.

Finally, like James himself, I am writing this book with Christians in mind. Most often the pronouns "we" or "us" refer to professing Christians. At the same time it is my hope that non-Christians reading this book will be helped and also persuaded to receive Christ as Lord and Savior.

For this reason, I have addressed that hope periodically throughout the book and have included a simple gospel presentation in the appendix (Becoming a Christian).

Enjoy!

Todd Linn, PhD
June 30, 2020

* * *

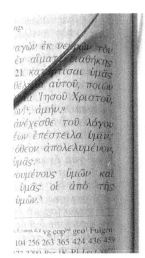

Introduction
(James 1:1)

1 James, a bondservant of God and of the Lord Jesus Christ, To the twelve tribes which are scattered abroad: Greetings.

James is a wonderfully practical book that challenges us to live out the Christian faith. It's a short book (a short letter really), just five chapters and one hundred and eight verses. It's also quite possibly the earliest book of the New Testament, written around AD 44-49. But big things come in small packages! James is action-packed, full of wisdom and challenge. It is also straightforward, honest, and often painful.

But before we go any further, just who is this guy named James? There are four men with the name James mentioned in the New Testament. There are James, "the son of Alphaeus," James, "the brother of John," James "the father of Jude," and then James "the brother of Jesus," often referred to as James "the Just."

It is this last James who is the writer of this letter; James the Just, or James "the brother of Jesus (Matthew 13:55)." Indeed it almost has to be this James for a number of reasons, among them the fact that this James was also leader of the Jerusalem church (Acts 15).

James is described as one of the pillars of the church in Jerusalem (Galatians 2:9), a leader of higher ranking than the Apostles Peter and John. That's a pretty big deal when you are in a leadership position over Peter and John!

So when we read this opening verse and it simply says, "James," without any other identifier, then it almost has to be "the" James, so to speak, because any other James would have had to distinguish himself, identifying himself as James "the son of Alphaeus," or James "the brother of John and son of Zebedee."

So the writer of the Book of James is *the* James. This is the leader of the council of Jerusalem in Acts 15, the very brother of Christ Himself, the one Paul wrote about his going up to see in Jerusalem, the one to whom he refers explicitly as "James, the Lord's brother (Galatians 1:19)."

Now that's remarkable, isn't it? The brother of Jesus; His little brother! Technically speaking, James is Christ's half-brother, of course. But James grew up in the same house as Jesus, sat at the same dinner table as Jesus, and played in the same yard as Jesus.

Of course James was not a believer in Jesus as Messiah in the earlier years of Jesus' ministry. John 7:5 says, "even His brothers did not believe in Him." Not surprising, really. I mean, how would you react if your brother—the very one you grew up with in the house—began to distinguish himself as Lord and Messiah?! James did, however, become a believer later, probably at the very moment Jesus singled him out for a special resurrection appearance (1 Corinthians 15:7).

That James believed Jesus to be Lord and God is evidenced in this opening verse where James refers to himself as both "bond-servant of God," and bondservant "of the Lord Jesus Christ." This latter descriptor is especially significant. The word James uses for Lord is the Greek word "kurios," a title of deity. It's the same word used throughout the Greek translation of the Old Testament with reference to the One True and Living God, the title used for "Elohim" and "Yahweh." Using the title here in James' letter, then, is tantamount to saying, "Jesus Christ is God."

So to whom is James writing? Well, verse 1 says he is writing to "the twelve tribes which are scattered abroad." The Greek literally reads the twelve tribes, "which are in the dispersion." The Jewish people, originally the 12 tribes of Israel, had been dispersed or scattered all over the world centuries earlier by the Assyrians and Babylonians. Now, in James' day, Jewish believers find themselves scattered again, this time scattered all over the Mediterranean world, largely as a result of opposition to their faith. So these are Jewish Christians gathering together in a number of "house churches" outside of Palestine.

Incidentally, the Book of James is considered one of the more "Jewish" letters of the New Testament, containing direct references or allusions to 22 books of the Old Testament (that's more than half of the Old Testament books), in addition to more than twenty allusions to Jesus' Sermon on the Mount (Matthew 5-7).

And while James has first century Jewish believers largely in view, the Bible is applicable to all persons in any age. All Scripture is God's Word. It is timeless, powerful and profitable to all who will read it and receive it's teachings (2 Timothy 3:16-17; Hebrews 4:12).

But be forewarned: James is not a book for the weak and timid! If you get squeamish when someone "tells it like it is," then James is probably not for you. If you want someone to sugar-coat difficult truths, then you will wince when you read James. James is continually "in our faces," calling for authentic, Christian living. James presents us with a "no-holds barred," straight-forward teaching of Christianity 101.

James addresses issues like spiritual snobbery in the church, worldliness among Christians, and unconcern for the poor and destitute. He rebukes us for our favoritism and addresses our use of the tongue; how we speak to others, how we speak about others. He is commanding!

In fact one of the more interesting characteristics of this letter is that it contains over fifty imperatives in its one hundred eight verses. Fifty uses of the imperative mood! The imperative is the mood of command. Statements such as, "Do this," or "Don't do that," are not suggestions, but commands.

For example, James says, "Be doers of the word, and not hearers only (James 1:22)." Other imperatives include: Don't show favoritism (James 2:1-4), submit to God, resist the devil (James 4:7), don't speak evil of another brother (James 4:11), and don't grumble against one another (James 5:9).

So the Book of James is about living the faith. When James uses the word "faith" in this letter (some sixteen times), he is stressing the practical *living-out* of Christian doctrine. His focus, then, is not so much upon our *becoming* a Christian as it is upon our *behaving* as a Christian. It is principles put into practice, or doctrine on display.

Like the title of this book, James wants us to "walk the walk." And if we don't walk the walk, James might say we're all talk, but no action. We're either walking the walk or just running our mouths!

As we begin our study let's see what James teaches about how we are to live when facing the reality of trials and hardships.

* * *

Chapter 1: When Facing Trials
(James 1:2-4)

2 My brethren, count it all joy when you fall into various trials,
3 knowing that the testing of your faith produces patience.
4 But let patience have its perfect work, that you may be perfect and complete, lacking nothing.

Every one of us is familiar with trials of one sort or other. And James is talking about *all* of them. He describes what he has in mind as "various trials" and by this he means to include any and all kinds of real or imagined trials. Trials are the storms we go through in life. It's often noted that every one of us has either gone *through* a storm, is presently *in* a storm, or getting ready to go through *another* storm.

Storms and trials are part of living in a sin-cursed and fallen world. Ever since our first parents (Adam and Eve) sinned in Genesis 3 we have experienced trials of one kind or another. We see evidence of the fall all around us. So while we are often shocked and saddened by tragic events, at the same time we are not surprised when they happen. We understand that this world is not as it was meant to be.

But trials hit home when we become personally involved in them. How helpful that we have passages such as this to encourage us as we go through them. Let's consider some practical truths that surface from these verses. First, note this:

Trials are Inevitable

That may sound rather obvious and perhaps even unhelpful, at first. But it is so important for us to remember this fact so we do not immediately fall into doubt or despair when trials come our way.

Too often when trials and hardships come we find ourselves immediately reacting by crying out, "God, why are You doing this to me?" And the implication is: "Surely, I don't *deserve* this misfortune!"

Rarely do we ever think to ask the *same* question when something favorable comes our way, or we are on the receiving end of some unforeseen good fortune: "God, why are You doing this to me? I don't deserve this success—give it to someone else!"

Truth is, we sinful human beings deserve nothing. The very air we breathe at this moment is an undeserved gift that comes graciously from our Creator. He can withhold the air if He wishes. He is God and we are not. But He is a good God and He always does what is right. So we trust Him, believing that He knows what He is doing and we take Him at His word when He teaches that trials and hardships actually serve not to harm us, but to help us. More about that in a moment.

For now let us consider that trials can come to anyone. Being a Christian does not keep one from trials. If you are a human being, you will go through trials. James does not say, "Count it all joy *if* you fall into various trials," but "*when* you fall into various trials."

In fact, the Bible teaches that Christians can expect to face suffering and hardships when others oppose their faith. For example, Jesus said, "In the world you will have tribulation (John 16:33)." The Apostle Paul warned: "All who desire to live godly in Christ Jesus will suffer persecution (2 Timothy 3:12)." And Peter wrote: "Beloved, do not think it strange concerning the fiery trial which is to try you, as though some strange thing happened to you (1 Peter 4:12)."

Trials are inevitable. And while the previous verses suggest more the idea of trials of persecution for one's faith, James has in view trials of any kind.

James was not himself immune from trials and suffering. Church history records that he died as a Christian martyr in the year AD 62. Josephus, the first-century Jewish historian, tells us that James was accused by the high priest and condemned to death by stoning.[1]

Eusebius, a fourth-century church historian, adds a few details about James' death. He says that the scribes and Pharisees took James to the top the temple, and "demanded that he should renounce the faith of Christ before all the people," but rather than deny Jesus, James "declared himself fully before the whole multitude, and confessed that Jesus Christ was the Son of God, our Savior and Lord."[2]

Another historian, Hegesippus, adds:

> They went up and threw down the just man [from the temple], and said to each other, "Let us stone James the Just." And they began to stone him, for he was not killed by the fall, but [James] knelt down and said, "I entreat thee, Lord God our Father, forgive them, for they know not what they do." One of them… took a club with which he beat [James] And thus he suffered martyrdom.[3]

So when we read James' describing the inevitability of trials, know that he himself is prepared to face them.

Again, trials can come to anyone. Being a Christian does not preclude one from facing danger, enduring suffering, or encountering hardships. If you are a human being, you will go through trials. And they may come suddenly and unexpectedly.

In fact the word "fall" in verse 2 is the same word used in Luke 10 where Jesus tells the parable of the Good Samaritan. Jesus says, "A certain man went down from Jerusalem to Jericho and *fell* among thieves (Luke 10:30)." This man was minding his own business and suddenly and unexpectedly he encountered thieves.

That is often just how suddenly trials arrive. We're minding our own business, the day starts off uneventfully and then we encounter one of a "variety" of trials, hardships, or difficulties.

Now James says that when this happens, we're to "count it all joy (verse 2)," or, "consider it joy." What exactly does this mean?

It does *not* mean that we are to consider the trial *itself* to be joyous. James does not say that. He is not calling for us to think, "Oh trials, how wonderful! I love trials and I am so joyful when they come!" That's a silly notion at best and a psychological disorder at worst.

He doesn't say, "count the *trials* joy," but rather, "count it all joy *when you fall into* various trials." This may sound at first like a distinction without a difference, but it is very different indeed. Reading on to verse 3, James continues: "knowing that the testing of your faith produces patience (or perseverance)."

Put another way: "Consider the fact that you are undergoing trials—painful as they may be—as an opportunity to grow in faith and become strong and, for that reason, you may have joy in the midst of your trials."

Here, then, James is arguing for another important and helpful truth:

Trials are Beneficial

Trials—painful as they may be—provide an opportunity to grow in Christian faith and become strong. In this way, trials are beneficial. They bring the benefit of strength and endurance to Christians. For this reason, we may have joy when facing them.

In fact, we rarely consider escaping a trial as a benefit *lost*. What do I mean? Well, let's be honest: If we pray without thinking, how do we usually pray about trials and hardships? Do we not usually fall into a sort of "default mode" of prayer, asking to escape the trial, or praying that we or the ones we love would never face any sort of trial at all?

A friend is sick and we pray that God heals her. A persecuted Christian is imprisoned so we pray for his release. And one of the reasons we do so is because we normally think only of the joy that comes in the *absence* of trials. To be sure, there is joy in sound health and religious freedom. No one disputes this. At the same time, however, James is calling for our rejoicing in the ability to benefit from the *presence* of trials and hardships.

James' stress is not on the joy we have when *escaping* trials, but on the joy we may have when *enduring* them. Indeed, one reason a Christian can be joyful when facing trials is because—as James puts it in verse 3—"the testing of our faith produces patience (or endurance)."

Trials strengthen us

Usually when I go to the gym I feel a bit inferior because I find myself in the presence of guys who have been working on their muscles for years and it shows. As I heard a friend once remark: "They have muscles in places I don't have places!"

But how do you get muscles? How do you grow strong? You "work out." And it *is* work. Muscles grow when they are tested.

It's like the guy who struggles to carry a load upon his shoulders. The first time is very difficult, but the longer he carries that load the stronger he becomes. Over time, he moves with greater ease and agility.

In the same way, the longer you carry the "load" of each trial, the stronger you become. Most Christians want to become strong in the faith. They really want to grow and mature. Well, think of God as your personal trainer who guides you through various "work out" routines because He knows what is best for your program of growth. And know that the longer you keep carrying the "weight" of your trials, God will strengthen you.

The word "patience" in verse 3 is a word that is better translated "endurance." It connotes the idea of standing strong in the presence of adversity.

Trials have a way of strengthening our trust in God as the One who always does what is right and knows what is best for us. It is often through the experience of painful trials that joy is discovered or enhanced.

John Piper helps us see this truth in his booklet, *Don't Waste Your Cancer.*[4] In the book, Piper (who was himself diagnosed with prostate cancer) helps Christians understand how God uses trials like cancer to draw us closer to Himself. And while Piper notes that praying for physical healing is certainly biblical and right, he also writes about the joy that can come in the midst of cancer, a God-focused joy that, if not experienced, might lead to one's cancer being lost or "wasted." Some of the points he brings out in the book include:

> You will waste your cancer if you fail to use it as a means of witness to the truth and glory of Christ.

> You will waste your cancer if you spend too much time reading about cancer and not enough time reading about God.

> You will waste your cancer if you think that "beating cancer"

means staying alive rather than cherishing Christ.

That last point is especially helpful. Our tendency is to think of "beating cancer" as the best goal, but the best goal is to cherish Christ and to be conformed to His image. So Piper reminds us:

Satan's and God's designs in your cancer are not the same. Satan designs to destroy your love for Christ. God designs to deepen your love for Christ. Cancer does not win if you die. It (only) wins if you fail to cherish Christ. God's design is to wean you off the breast of the world and feast you on the sufficiency of Christ. It is meant to help you say and feel, "I count everything as loss because of the surpassing worth of knowing Christ Jesus as my Lord." And to know that therefore, "To live is Christ, and to die is gain (Philippians 3:8; Philippians 1:21)."

Cancer doesn't win, nor does any trial or affliction win, unless we value our temporary human existence over and above cherishing Christ, and growing in Christ, and becoming more complete in Christ Jesus.

This takes us to another benefit of trials:

Trials complete us

In verse 4 James teaches that once endurance has "its perfect work" or, we may say, "has done its job" then, writes James, "you may be perfect (or mature) and complete, lacking nothing."

"Mature" and "complete." In other words, apart from trials, we are "immature" and "incomplete." That's why you can count it all joy when you fall into various trials, because they present to you an opportunity to grow, to grow up in your faith and to become more like Jesus Christ. You can't become mature and complete if you never suffer. Trials strengthen us and trials complete us.

You really can't become like Christ apart from suffering.

Without trials we could never really learn humility or genuine love.

Couples who have been married for years have a deeper love for one another precisely because they have been through difficult times together. A young couple who thinks they're ready to marry and have known each other only a short time haven't even had a chance to fight yet! It is through difficulties and challenges that love really matures and grows.

Without trials we could never really learn patience, or wisdom.

Through trials, we become more and more like Christ. The Apostle Paul teaches as much in Romans 8:28-29: "God works all things together for good to those who love God, to those who are the called according to His purpose, for whom He foreknew, He also predestined to be conformed to the image of His Son..."

God works all things together for the good of completing us, conforming us more greatly to the image of His Son, Jesus Christ.

Think of it: without trials we are less like Christ. Without trials we are immature, underdeveloped. Without trials we are incomplete. Without trials we could never really learn compassion or empathy.

Paul teaches in 2 Corinthians chapter 1, for example, that God comforts us in our trials and difficulties so that we may be in a position to comfort others in their trials and difficulties with the same comfort that we ourselves have received from God (2 Corinthians 1:3-4). That's compassion; that's empathy.

Paul wrote as one who had faced numerous hardships and difficulties. Have you read of his "thorn in the flesh?" Paul had some kind of affliction. Nobody knows exactly what it was, but he wrote about it in 2 Corinthians chapter 12. Calling it a "thorn in the flesh," Paul described it as that which was beneficial to him. Given what he had written in 2 Corinthians 2 about our being in a position to comfort others as a result of our own trials, Paul surely was able to see that his affliction served to strengthen him, complete him, and equip him with the ability to bless others in their trials and afflictions.

Theologian Wayne Grudem sees God's wisdom in His assigning Paul his "thorn in the flesh." Defining God's wisdom as His "always choosing the best goals and the best means to those goals," Grudem asserts:

> It should be our great confidence and a source of peace day by day to know that God causes all things to move us toward the ultimate goal He has for our lives, namely, that we might be like Christ and thereby giving glory to Him. Such confidence enabled Paul to accept his "thorn in the flesh" (2 Corinthians 12:7) as something that, though painful, God in His wisdom had chosen not to remove (2 Corinthians 12:8-10).[5]

God in His wisdom knows what He is doing. Small wonder that James goes on to say in the very next verse, verse 5, "If any of you *lacks* wisdom, let him ask of God..." We'll talk more about that in the next chapter!

What About You?

While it is right to pray for deliverance from trials, James does not call for this, but rather for our rejoicing when we fall into them. Why?

"Truth is, we sinful human beings deserve nothing." Do you agree with this statement? Why or why not? Be sure to support your answer from Scripture.

In what ways can you become more "complete" or "mature" as a result of your present hardships and difficulties?

❊ ❊ ❊

Chapter 2: Wisdom for Troubled Times
(James 1:5-8)

5 If any of you lacks wisdom, let him ask of God, who gives to all liberally and without reproach, and it will be given to him.
6 But let him ask in faith, with no doubting, for he who doubts is like a wave of the sea driven and tossed by the wind.
7 For let not that man suppose that he will receive anything from the Lord;
8 he is a double-minded man, unstable in all his ways.

Years ago before my oldest son was born I began a project to restore a bedroom chest of drawers that belonged to me when I was small and had also belonged to my father when he was small. So I wanted to complete this project before my son was born so that we could place it in the nursery and he would have it growing up. But it needed a lot of work. And so I stored the chest of drawers in my landlord's woodshed and I'd go over there after work each evening and work on it.

It still had this strange blend of colors that had been painted on it, popular in the early 70s, a mixture of green and brown swirls all over it. And I wanted to strip it down to its original wood and just stain it so all the paint had to be removed along with, as I discovered much to my dismay, another color of paint underneath it.

After the paint was removed I had to remove a bit of the ruined wood near the bottom of the chest of drawers where it had gotten wet, a bit of unwanted and splintered wood at the base. I had to remove it and then sand away the rough edges. In fact, the sanding was some of the most grueling work. It took a long time to sand the entire piece of furniture, smoothing out all the rough spots before it was ready to have a new coat of stain applied to it.

While the piece was unfinished it looked pretty rough. I didn't have a lot of time to work on it so it sat incomplete in my landlord's shed for some weeks and months. He was eager for me to finish the job, but I only had so much time after work each day to devote to it. So it sat in the shed incomplete for many weeks waiting for me to finish it.

When it was finally finished I have to say that it looked really good! In fact it still looks good and both of my boys have benefited from having it in their respective rooms as they grew up in our home.

In many ways James is teaching us that God is doing a work in our lives that is largely incomplete until He has finished His perfect work of restoration. And just like a piece of furniture, God often has to first "strip us down," allowing trials into our lives to remove some of the rough edges of our personalities or the unwanted shards and splinters of our erroneous thinking. He breaks off all the unwanted stuff that doesn't look like Jesus as He tests and strengthens our faith. He sands and smoothes and ultimately restores us into something beautiful, conforming us to the glorious image of His Son (Romans 8:28-29).

In the last chapter, we read where James made this very point in verse 4: "But let patience (or endurance) have its perfect work (or its full effect), that you may be perfect (mature) and complete, lacking nothing."

And so James now writes in verse 5, "(and) If any of you lacks wisdom, let him ask of God," which is to say, "If this work I am doing in your life, 'stripping away and sanding you' through trials of adversity and difficulty, if this does not seem to make sense to you and you lack wisdom, ask of Me and I will help you out."

God provides wisdom for troubled times. There is power available to us as we persevere through hardships and difficulties. In these verses James tell us *what* to do, *how* to do it, and what happens if we do it *wrong.* First:

What to Do:
Ask God for wisdom

God gives His wisdom generously to all who ask Him. James says we need only "Ask of God." Note that carefully. Ask of *God.* He is the One to whom you go. He is the One to whom we pray. The Bible never says, "Ask of Mary" or, "Ask of Saint Monica," to pray along with you. Ask of God.

The NIV puts it this way: "If any of you lacks wisdom, you should ask God, who gives generously to all without finding fault, and it will be given to you."

Ask God for wisdom. And if you ask Him, here is the promise: He will give it. He will give wisdom generously to all who ask Him. He will not rebuke anyone for asking. He'll not say something like: "What are *you* doing here asking me for wisdom?!" He will not turn anyone away who asks for wisdom.

And God has an infinite supply of wisdom. Paul declares: "Oh, the depth of the riches of the wisdom and knowledge of God (Romans 11:33a)!" So we need only ask of God and He will gladly give to us because He always has a rich supply in store.

Incidentally, verse 5 is often cited apart from its context. Make no mistake: it *will* stand on its own. In faith, we can ask God for wisdom no matter our need and God is glad to oblige us. So you can ask God for wisdom when you are struggling with a problem, trying to figure something out, for example. It may not be a particular trial or hardship, but you're just trying to solve a solution at work or something similar and you ask God for wisdom.

But the real effect of this verse is found in the context of what James has just said about trials, hardships, difficulties and affliction. It is in the context of God's working in our lives, testing us, strengthening us, chipping away all the stuff that doesn't look like Jesus, stripping us down in order to "finish us," mature us, and complete us. It is in *this* context that James says, "Now by the way, if you are having a hard time persevering through the trials, and you need help seeing things as God sees them, then just ask for wisdom and God will give it to you."

Someone said that wisdom is the ability to see our circumstances from God's perspective. I like that idea—even if I can't exactly see the way that God sees—because I am reminded that God is working through our circumstances, conforming us into Christlikeness.

So what are we to do if we need wisdom during troubled times? We ask of God. That's *what* to do. Next:

How to Do it:
Ask in faith, with no doubting

James writes, "But let him ask in faith, without doubting."

Now at first that may sound impossible! After all, don't we all doubt? We struggle with doubts all the time.

It seems that what James wants us to do is to determine whether our trust is really in God or perhaps in something (or someone) else. We often say we trust God. It would seem James is challenging us to consider whether we *really* trust God or whether we just *say* we trust God.

Do we trust God at the first and then begin to waver? Do we trust God at the first, but then begin to rely upon our own abilities or our own reasoning? James goes on to say that when we respond this way we are like a wave of the sea tossed about.

The New Living Translation of verse 6 is helpful: "But when you ask him, be sure that your faith is in God alone. Do not waver, for a person with divided loyalty is as unsettled as a wave of the sea that is blown and tossed by the wind."

We are to have an undivided faith, a settled trust in God, a belief that He is at work and that He always does what is right. So we must not waver. We must continue to stand firm in our reliance upon God.

When we "doubt" we are in essence saying, "God, I'm not sure I really trust You. I'm not sure I really believe that You are in control and that You always do what is right." When we think this way we are beginning to rest upon our own reasoning rather than resting upon God. This is the principle taught in Proverbs 3 that many know and love:

> *Trust in the Lord with all your heart*
>   *and lean not on your own understanding;*
> *in all your ways submit to him,*
>   *and he will make your paths straight.*
> *Do not be wise in your own eyes;*
>   *fear the Lord and shun evil.*
> *This will bring health to your body*
>   *and nourishment to your bones*
>   (Proverbs 3:5-8; NIV)

Rather than attempting to be "wise in our own eyes," we are to trust in the Lord with all of our heart. Solomon warns: "Don't lean upon your own reasoning." Reason, yes! Think, yes! But don't *lean* upon your own understanding, don't rely solely upon it. Rather, fear the Lord, which brings health to your body and nourishment to your bones.

This brings us to James' final consideration regarding wisdom for troubled times. We have read about *what* to do (ask God for wisdom), *how* to do it (ask in faith, with no doubting), and now:

What Happens if You Do it Wrong
You'll be unstable in all your ways

Not trusting in God, but placing our trust somewhere else, such as relying on own abilities, makes us unstable. We'll be unstable "in all our ways" like aimless waves of the sea driven by the wind, moving one way then another, carried about with little sense of peace or purpose.

James also gives another illustration of what happens when we say we trust in the Lord, but then doubt Him by trusting in ourselves or relying exclusively upon some other counsel. He says we become a "double-minded man." What a picture! Literally, it is to have "two minds," one about God and one about something else. It is to have a willingness on the one hand to trust in God, but then to doubt God by trusting in human reason, or natural abilities, and so on.

And the reason this is so problematic is that by our doubting we are indicating we are unsure about God's goodness and character. Think about it: When are you most likely to doubt God's goodness and character? Isn't it when you are going through especially difficult trials? We are vulnerable to wrong ways of thinking when we suffer hardships, difficulties, and affliction. During those times we may doubt God's goodness.

It's easier to talk about the goodness of God and His gracious abounding love and mercy when we're *not* going through any hardships. But when the trials come, we must remember the goodness of God. We must remember the character of God, that He always does what is right. Otherwise we begin to doubt His character and attempt to mix our faith in God with our own reason, or our own abilities, or the advice of others.

When I was small I remember watching a game show called the Hollywood Squares. It was a kind of Tic-Tac-Toe game where Hollywood movie stars or personalities each occupied a square and the stars were asked questions by the host. After the star answered—and sometimes it was the right answer, sometimes a bluff, and sometimes the wrong answer—the host would then ask the contestant, "Do you agree or disagree?"

And then the contestant would weigh what he heard and judge the veracity of the star's answer. Maybe the contestant felt he knew better than the star and he might respond, "Disagree," or maybe he didn't know the answer and was banking on the star's knowledge and so he'd reply, "Agree." And the host would look on his card and say whether the star had answered the question correctly.

Some people treat God like He's a star in the game show Hollywood Squares. They want His input so they open His Word and God speaks, but they want to weigh the veracity of what He has said against their own experience. They want to weigh God's Word against their own knowledge or their own feelings. And so, while God has spoken, they may respond, "I disagree." James says they are double-minded, trying to mix Godly wisdom with worldly wisdom.

Where does this kind of thinking lead? It leads to instability. I don't know anyone who actually wants to be "unstable in all his ways," but this is precisely what happens when we choose to go against God.

In closing, let's consider a few ways that God grants His wisdom to us when we encounter troubled times. God grants wisdom primarily in four ways: through His Word (the Bible), through prayer, through the Holy Spirit, and through wise Christians. Of course, these are not the *only* ways God grants wisdom, but these are, in my estimation, the primary ways God grants wisdom.

God's Word

If you are wanting God's wisdom you must have a regular daily time of Bible reading. The Bible is not just an ancient near eastern book full of sage advice. The Bible is God's Word. We must read it regularly if we hope to have something of the wisdom of God.

Before you read the Bible pray this simple prayer: "God, open Your Word to me and open me to Your Word." Listen to God speak to you as you read His Word and you will be strengthened to stand in the face of adversity. As Charles Spurgeon once said, "A Bible that's falling apart usually belongs to someone who isn't."

Prayer

This is the most obvious way as it is given in verse 5: "Ask of God." Pray. Talk to God. James knew something about talking to God. Church history records James as having the nickname "old camel knees." In other words, his knees had become so tough and calloused from kneeling in prayer that they looked like the knees of a camel.

Pray every day. Pray in the morning. Pray throughout the day. And especially when you find yourself in the midst of troubled times, talk to the Lord. It's right here in the text: "If any of you lacks wisdom, let him ask of God."

Holy Spirit

If you are a Christian, you have the Holy Spirit within you (1 Corinthians 6:19-20; Ephesians 1:13). God is in you to guide you and lead you along. And the Bible says in Ephesians 5:18 that we are to be "filled" with the Spirt. I like to be aware of His presence. Often I will bow my head, close my eyes, and I'll say, "Spirit, fill me. Take complete control of my life."

And especially in these times when we are going through hardships we are wise to bow our heads, close our eyes, and say, "Spirit, fill me. Take control of my life" and God will guide us. He will lead us to think, to speak, and to do, what is right.

Wise Christians

We get by with a little help from our friends, Christian friends. Don't misunderstand: non-Christian friends can help too, but wise Christian friends are a particular source of strength because they will counsel us from the Word of God. Their counsel squares with God's truth (or at least, it *should*!).

Wise Christians are found in our local church (the most immediate and most important location) as well as other places. Good books, for example—books written by wise Christians, full of Scripture and sound theology—help us weather the storms of life.

Wisdom for troubled times can also come through sermons, preachers on the radio or podcasts, or other Christians—wise, growing Christians—Christians with whom we worship or Christians in our small group get togethers.

These are the primary means by which God grants wisdom: the Bible, prayer, the Holy Spirit, and wise Christians. We must avail ourselves to each of these means consistently if we hope to grow in wisdom.

What About You?

How significant is the context in which verse 5 is found (following James' teaching about trials)?

What do you think causes us to doubt the goodness of God?

Of the four primary ways God grants wisdom, which needs a little more attention in your life?

❋ ❋ ❋

Chapter 3: Trials of Poverty & Prosperity
(James 1:9-12)

9 Let the lowly brother glory in his exaltation,
10 but the rich in his humiliation, because as a flower of the field he will pass away.
11 For no sooner has the sun risen with a burning heat than it withers the grass; its flower falls, and its beautiful appearance perishes. So the rich man also will fade away in his pursuits.
12 Blessed is the man who endures temptation (or trials); *for when he has been approved, he will receive the crown of life which the Lord has promised to those who love Him.*

I f there is one thing we have learned so far as we have studied the first few verses of James' letter it is that trials are inevitable. Every one of us can expect to fall into some kind of hardship, difficulty, trial or trouble.

We have also noted that the ultimate purpose for which God allows us to fall into various trials and hardships is to perfect us, or to mature us, completing us. In a word, to make us more like Jesus. So without the trials and hardships, what are we? We are immature. We are incomplete. We require still further work before God is finished with us.

When you cook a meal or bake a cake you mix everything up and put it in the oven and set the timer. Time passes and then you hear the timer go off. You go and look into the oven at what you are making and it looks good, it looks like it's done. But you don't really know until you stick a fork into it or, in the case of a cake, a toothpick into it to see whether it is really done. Because on the *outside* it looks done, but you really don't know because you can't see the *inside* and it may require a little more time before it is *complete*, and *perfect, lacking nothing*.

James is teaching that God is doing a work in your life like that. And often we go through the oven of various trials and troubles. The "heat is on" as we often say. And the work God is doing is not always obvious on the outside because God's work is done primarily on the inside. God is doing a work on the inside of us, building character within us, teaching us how to stand in the face of adversity. So He knows how things are going inside of us and He knows how much more time we need to become mature, complete, lacking nothing.

James then discusses two trials in which Christians may find themselves, trials of poverty and prosperity.

Perhaps we're not prepared to place both of these situations in the same category. We may see *poverty* as a trial; that seems clear enough, but if poverty and prosperity are *both* considered hardships, we may think, "Give me the trial of prosperity! I think I can handle the trial of wealth, so bring it on!"

But the trial of prosperity may be more difficult to overcome than we think, especially if we live in a prosperous country. If trials are regarded especially challenging because we have difficulty getting through them—acknowledging our temptation to take our eyes off Christ and look elsewhere, relying upon the world rather than the Lord—then perhaps we can see how easily we may stumble when we find ourselves in a trial of prosperity. It's a matter of perspective.

Stay Focused with a Heavenly Perspective

A recurring theme in James' letter is the division between heavenly thinking and worldly thinking. We will see him flesh out this teaching more fully as we progress through his letter. He warns later for example: "Friendship with the world is enmity with God. Whoever therefore wants to be a friend of the world makes himself an enemy of God (James 4:4)."

Christians must guard against their natural, fallen tendency to have a worldly perspective of success. This is especially true regarding money and material possessions.

God honors the poor (showing true prosperity)

James writes, "Let the lowly brother glory in his exaltation."

Contextually we see that verse 9 is meant to be contrasted with verse 10 where James addresses the rich. So we know that this word "lowly" or "lowly brother" in verse 9 has to do with "low economic condition," or poverty.

In James' day there really was no middle class. For the most part, one was either rich or poor. So if a Christian were poor he may be tempted to think, "Well, I'm just the lowest rung on the ladder in this world." Yet James comes along and says, "Hey, God sees this thing entirely differently and you need to see your situation entirely differently, too. You're looking at your situation from the wrong vantage point, you have merely a worldly perspective."

From a heavenly perspective, no Christian occupies the lowest rung on the ladder! Christians have a very high position. This is the sense of James' exhortation in verse 9: "Let the lowly brother glory in his exaltation." God honors the poor Christian, showing him his *true* wealth, his *true* prosperity, his spiritual riches in Christ.

If you are a Christian who is poor, remember that you are Christian who is rich! You may be poor from a worldly perspective, but you are rich from a heavenly perspective. What could be better than to be saved from the penalty of sin and to gain an eternal inheritance? You are spiritually wealthy!

James' teaching is similar to Paul's teaching elsewhere:

> Our light affliction, which is but for a moment, is working for us a far more exceeding and eternal weight of glory, while we do not look at the things which are seen, but at the things which are not seen. For the things which are seen are temporary, but the things which are not seen are eternal (2 Corinthians 4:17-18).

Stay focused with a heavenly perspective. Don't stumble and fall through your trial of poverty by thinking you are on the lowest rung of the ladder when you are actually on the highest rung of the ladder.

In the same way, James turns his attention to the rich and warns them. It is as though James were saying, "And you guys who are rich, you also be sure to keep a heavenly perspective. Be sure to view your riches with eternity in mind and, when you do that, you won't expect your riches to last and you won't look to your riches for ultimate security and ultimate happiness."

This is probably the greater challenge for most of us reading this book. Most of us are very wealthy compared to global standards of living. Most American Christians are doing very well by worldly metrics. So if the "lowly brother" is to "glory in his *exaltation* (verse 9)," we read now in verse 10: "but the rich in his *humiliation*."

God humbles the rich (showing true poverty)

See how James address both rich and poor insofar as trials are concerned? The wise Christian understands that God works through both trials of poverty and prosperity to strengthen faith, to strengthen trust, to strengthen our dependence upon Him.

James teaches here that the rich Christian should glory (or thank God for) not his *exaltation*, which is what we may have expected if we were thinking in purely secular or worldly terms, but in his *humiliation*, his low standing from God's viewpoint, from a heavenly perspective.

Too many of us are tempted to believe that riches are everything: "Get riches and you're on top of the world!" This faulty thinking creeps into the church, even the most conservative, Bible-believing, Christ-honoring churches.

Some self-examination may be helpful here. Do you have a greater tendency to desire to be around *wealthy* Christians or *poor* Christians? Don't answer too quickly here, just be honest with yourself. Do you hope some of the "worldly success" of the rich rubs off on you or that your status may be somehow elevated if you are around them?

James teaches that those who have much don't have as much as we may think. What they *have* may pass away in a moment, or *they* may pass away in a moment. This is the point of verses 10 and following. James says the rich Christian—the wise, rich Christian—humbles himself by understanding that a dependence upon his worldly riches is wrong because his life is relatively short and unpredictable.

Of course what is true for the rich person is true for every person. Every person will die. Compared to eternity, our lives are short whether we live to be a hundred years old or older. The duration of our lives is like a beautiful summer day when the sun is shining and it is warm and we smile and everything feels just right but then, in a moment, "no sooner has the sun risen with a burning heat than it withers the grass; its flower falls, and its beautiful appearance perishes."

James is speaking metaphorically, which means he's talking not so much about the *grass* dying suddenly as he is talking about *people* dying suddenly, *Christians* dying suddenly. And not just *poor* Christians dying suddenly, but also *rich* Christians dying suddenly. His teaching here is similar to the question he asks later in chapter 4: "For what is your life? It is even a vapor that appears for a little time and then vanishes away (James 4:14)."

See the great tragedy in a person's living merely for riches! Christians must hold onto their wealth loosely, knowing the joy of giving to others, giving to the church, giving to support missionaries, and other kingdom work.

True poverty is not having *little* in this world. True poverty is not even having *much* in this world. True poverty is having *much* in this world and living *only for* this world.

So often James sounds like his half-brother, Jesus. Jesus taught this same way of regarding material things in His Sermon on the Mount:

> Do not lay up for yourselves treasures on earth, where moth and rust destroy and where thieves break in and steal; but lay up for yourselves treasures in heaven, where neither moth nor rust destroys and where thieves do not break in and steal. For where your treasure is, there your heart will be also (Matthew 6:19-21).

James frequently echoes the teachings of Christ. In fact his letter contains no fewer than twenty-six allusions to the words of Jesus. Even James' teaching on the "double-minded man (James 1:8)," sounds a bit like our Lord's teaching on divided loyalties:

> "No one can serve two masters; for either he will hate the one and love the other, or else he will be loyal to the one and despise the other. You cannot serve God and [money]."—Matthew

6:24

When it comes to trials of poverty and prosperity, we must maintain a heavenly perspective. And there is something else here:

Stand Firm for a Heavenly Promise

We noted earlier that God means to work through our trials and hardships, testing our faith, strengthening our faith so that we may be perfect, or complete, mature, and lacking nothing. God means to work through our trials to make us more like Jesus, more greatly conformed to Christlikeness.

James now reminds Christians that their persevering through trials and hardships culminates in their receiving a "crown of life," a crown "the Lord has promised to those who love Him."

So no matter how great the trial, remember where you are headed. One day you will receive a crown, not an earthly crown, a worldly crown given to winners of athletic games. Nor will you receive a mere golden crown, such as those worn by earthly kings. Rather, you will receive the "crown of life which the Lord has promised to those who love Him." This "crown" is not so much a thing to be worn as a life to be lived—eternal life. It is a life that is given to us through faith in Jesus Christ, a life we begin to live in this world now, but a life that is enjoyed long after we die, a life that finds its greatest expression in the final state of heaven.

There is a reward awaiting Christians who keep the faith and persevere during trials. There is a promise from God to be fulfilled one day, a promise God makes to Christians who stand fast in the face of hardships and difficulties. Stay focused on Christ and stand firm in your trials and one day you will receive the "crown of life."

As Paul writes in Romans 8:18: "For I consider that the sufferings of this present time are not worthy to be compared with the glory which shall be revealed in us."

What About You?

What do you think is easier for a Christian to handle: riches or poverty? Why?

Would you describe your financial stewardship as "close-fisted" or "open-handed?"

Are you certain you will one day receive the "crown of life?" On what basis?

Chapter 4: Tackling Temptation
(James 1:13-18)

13 Let no one say when he is tempted, "I am tempted by God"; for God cannot be tempted by evil, nor does He Himself tempt anyone.
14 But each one is tempted when he is drawn away by his own desires and enticed.
15 Then, when desire has conceived, it gives birth to sin; and sin, when it is full-grown, brings forth death.
16 Do not be deceived, my beloved brethren.
17 Every good gift and every perfect gift is from above, and comes down from the Father of lights, with whom there is no variation or shadow of turning.
18 Of His own will He brought us forth by the word of truth, that we might be a kind of firstfruits of His creatures.

One evening after worship I went into the office of a church I served and made a delightful discovery: someone had anonymously given me an entire box of donuts! There was a nice card, yet nicer still was the variety of donuts in the box: chocolate, vanilla, strawberry-iced, assorted cake donuts and creme-filled donuts. I have a sweet tooth and this gift made my night!

As I recall, most of them were gone before bedtime. I had given at least one away earlier, but my family ate the rest. And when I say, "my family" I mean mostly "me." Oh I didn't eat all of them myself, but I ate far more than I should have.

Now I could reason, "Well, you know, I *deserved* those donuts. After all, they were given to me and the person who gave them intended that I enjoy them." Yes, but they probably did not intend that I enjoy them all at once.

Truth is, I allowed my desire for something good to be an occasion for temptation. James says, "Each one is tempted when he is drawn away by his own desires and enticed." My eating too many donuts was not the anonymous giver's fault. Eating too many donuts was nobody's fault but my own.

To be sure, my consuming too many donuts may be thought a relatively minor offense, not unlike the little boy whose mother caught him in the kitchen with his hand in the cookie jar. She thundered: "What are you doing?!" And he replied, "I'm fighting temptation!"

With such levity I certainly don't mean to overshadow the seriousness of greater temptations, I'm just not willing to describe my own in this book. Of this much we may be certain: whatever the source and substance of our temptations, James indicates that the pattern is always the same: "Each one is tempted when he is drawn away by his own desires and enticed."

In fact, James provides no fewer than three facts we must know about temptation. First:

Know the Cause of Temptation

James cautions: "Let no one say when he is tempted, 'I am tempted by God.'"[6] In other words, don't blame God. God is not the cause of temptation. When you are battling temptation, whether it is a temptation to overeat, to drink, to use drugs, to look lustfully at someone, to insult another, to strike another —whatever your temptation—don't blame God. He is not the cause of temptation.

Not only is God not the cause of temptation, but He Himself "cannot be tempted by evil." We know this to be true of God if we have a biblical theology of God. The Bible teaches that God is all-sufficient. There's nothing He needs, nothing He desires, nothing He craves. So God cannot be tempted by evil. He is completely satisfied in Himself and is all-sufficient.

And James adds, "Nor does He Himself tempt anyone." Why? Because God does not delight in sin. He's not going to tempt anyone to do evil. He hates evil. God is not the cause of our temptation.

Does this truth keep us from blaming God? No. The "blame game" was played first in the Garden of Eden (Genesis 3). Our first parents (Adam and Eve) played the blame game. They both succumbed to the temptation to eat the forbidden fruit from the Tree of Life. Afterwards, God confronted Adam and Adam blamed Eve. He also blamed God! Remember what Adam said? "The woman...You gave me! She made me do it!" Then God confronted Eve and Eve blamed the serpent.

Will Rogers used to say there were two eras in history: the passing of the buffalo and the passing of the buck. Blaming others, or "passing the buck," is part of our sin nature. We are, after all, Adam's children.

No, we cannot blame God for being the cause of our temptation. So who *is* to blame? James teaches that the cause of temptation does not originate with God, but with us—or better still, *within* us. He writes that "each one is tempted when he is drawn away by his own desires and enticed."

Sin is always an inside job. Sin begins in the heart. Each one is tempted when he is drawn away by his own desires, often wrong desires, or misplaced desires. We sin only when we allow ourselves to be "drawn away" by these desires and then "enticed." We must recognize these desires for what they are and immediately renounce them. If we will do that, we will avoid being "enticed" and led into sin. Therefore, yielding to temptation is nobody's fault but our own. Rather than blaming our actions on others—including the devil—we must own our actions.

Like the construction worker during his lunch break at the job site. He opens up his lunch box and says, "Oh, no! Baloney sandwich again! Four out five days this week it's been a baloney sandwich. If I see another baloney sandwich, I'm gonna be sick!" His construction worker buddy says, "Well, why don't you ask your wife to pack you something else?" And he says, "Oh, I'm not married. I pack it myself."

At least he owned his actions! The cause of temptation is an inside job. We must realize that we have within us the ability to be drawn away by our wrong or misplaced desires. If we yield to those desires, we will be "enticed" and will fall into sin.

Owning our actions is to acknowledge that we can avoid sin. We are not powerlessly drawn away and enticed by something beyond our control. Someone has said, "You can't keep birds from flying over your head, but you can keep them from building a nest in your hair." So true!

In a moment we'll consider behaviors that will help us respond correctly to temptation, lessening the likelihood of our yielding to it. Before we do that, let's feel the full force of James' warning by considering a word picture for the words "drawn away" and "enticed." They are both words that convey ideas from fishing or hunting. They are the same words used to describe the "baiting" of something, like baiting a trap or baiting a fish hook. To be "drawn away" is to be "lured" as by a fishing lure.

Few fish will bite a hook if there's nothing on it. So if you're wanting to catch a fish, you cover up the hook with some kind of bait. The bait hides the hook. So the fish comes along and sees the bait. He doesn't see the hook. The fish swims up to the bait and finds the bait attractive. The fish is "drawn away by his own desires and enticed." The fish has taken the bait. And what does the fish now discover? Underneath that bait is the snare of the hook. And all at once it is all over for the fish. Too late to turn back. The hook is set and the fish is caught.

It's one thing to talk about fish and quite another to talk about men and women, but the pattern is the same. Once we allow ourselves to be drawn away by our desires, it is just a matter of time before the hook is set and we have entered into sin.

Now this leads us to the next fact James wants us to know about temptation. We have considered first the cause of temptation. Next:

Know the Consequence of Temptation

Once we allow ourselves to be drawn away by our desires and enticed, James warns: "then, when desire has conceived, it gives birth to sin; and sin, when it is full-grown, brings forth death."

Remember: this all takes place within each person. Again, sin is an inside job. See how it works in one of the most familiar accounts in the Old Testament: King David, a godly man once described as a man after God's own heart (1 Samuel 13:14; Acts 13:22).

We read in 2 Samuel 11 that King David stays at home during a season when kings are generally found on the battlefield. The Bible says that one evening David walks out on his rooftop to have a look around. And from this vantage point he happens to see a young woman bathing herself. Now, had David just turned away and gone back inside, that would have been the end of it. But he didn't. He kept looking, watching this young woman;

Bathsheba, watching her as she bathed herself.

His perpetual looking was not Bathsheba's fault. The text suggest she is completely unaware of his watching her. It was David's fault to continue looking. And the more he looks, the more he thinks and the more he feels. Desire is forming within. And the longer he looks at this unsuspecting woman—a married woman as he will soon learn—the more greatly David allows himself to be "drawn away by his own desire and enticed." Remember what James writes next? "When desire has conceived, it gives birth to sin."

David calls for Bathsheba and she is brought to the king's palace. Given his royal position and the expected compliance of all persons under his authority, we shouldn't be too surprised by Bathsheba's willingness to follow the king's directives. The writer's economy of words is understandable: "Then David sent messengers, and took her; and she came to him, and he lay with her...and she returned to her house (2 Samuel 11:4)."

Many today would consider David's actions to be nothing more than a "fling," an affair, or a one-night stand. The Bible calls it a sin, namely the sin of adultery. And, as is often the case with such egregious sins, the duration of the sin was remarkably short compared to the years of consequences that followed.

James asserts: "When desire has conceived, it gives birth to sin; and sin, when it is full-grown, brings forth death." James is writing metaphorically and yet, in David's case, this literally happened. The child conceived by Bathsheba dies as a consequence of David's sin, discipline by God. And the death of the child was certainly a painful consequence for both David and Bathsheba. And yet a fate far worse than physical death was the death of David's vigor and spirit for the rest of his days. He is clearly a broken man after his adultery. He is not the man he once was. He is broken; broken by sin and temptation.

Little wonder James cautions, "Do not be deceived, my beloved brethren." Never think that you can give in to a particular temptation "just once" and all will be well. We must never toy with temptation. Learn from David! Do not flirt with others. Don't click on questionable web links. Don't look at the picture. Don't watch the video. Don't even joke about sin. Listen again to James' warning: "Do not be deceived, my beloved brethren."

Here is a reminder that we are all capable of being deceived. Just as trials are inevitable, so temptation is inevitable. Remember that James writes, "Let no one say *when* (not if) he is tempted…" Every Christian is subject to temptation. As Paul warns elsewhere, "Let him who thinks he stands take heed lest he fall (1 Corinthians 10:12)."

Thankfully, God provides the means of escape from every temptation. Paul goes on to say in the very next verse, "No temptation has overtaken you except such as is common to man; but God is faithful, who will not allow you to be tempted beyond what you are able, but with the temptation will also make the way of escape, that you may be able to bear it (1 Corinthians 10:13)."

This happy consideration takes us to the next fact Christians should know about temptation. We have read of the cause of temptation and the consequences of temptation. Finally:

Know the Correction for Temptation

Perhaps the correction seems as easy as just saying "No" to temptation. Isn't that all there is to it? Just stop, don't look, don't go there?

Saying "No" certainly is necessary, but this action alone is incomplete. We must not only say, "No" to something, we must also say "Yes" to something—or better, *Someone*.

When Christians give in to temptation they are allowing themselves to be drawn away by wrong or misplaced desires. These desires are substitutes for the only thing that can completely satisfy our inner yearnings: a vibrant, sustaining, relationship with our Lord Jesus Christ. So while saying "No" to wrong desires is necessary, it is equally necessary to say "Yes" to right desires. We avoid the "badness" of sin by delighting in the goodness of God.

Delight in God's goodness

James writes, "Every good gift and every perfect gift is from above, and comes down from the Father of lights, with whom there is no variation or shadow of turning."

Directing our gaze upward, James describes God as the, "Father of lights," the one "with whom there is no variation or shadow of turning."

There is some helpful theology here. The word "variation" James uses is an astronomical term. Unlike the ever-changing lights that move across the earth as it rotates on its axis creating "variation" of sun rays and moon beams that result in "shifting shadows," the Heavenly Father of lights, the God who *created* the lights, He *never changes*.

God is constantly the same, perfect in all of His ways. He never changes, which means He always does what is right and always acts in good ways. You can count on Him to be there always and to be faithful always. He is always *doing* good things and *providing* good things for His children.

Why do you think James places this truth at this point in the text? Given the context, it would seem James is teaching that the correction for temptation is theological. This verse reminds us of the character and nature of God. He is consistently good. He is not temptation's *cause,* He is temptation's *cure.* He is the correction for temptation.

So rather than settling for a bad gift, the gift that comes in the form of a baited hook, delight in the goodness of God. Say "No" to sin—that's half of it—and to the other half, say "Yes" to God.

Reject the broken cistern of murky water—your temptation to sin—and drink from the well that never shall run dry. Turn to God.

Delighting in God's goodness means enjoying the abundance of good things He gives to His children. He gives good gifts like satisfaction, joy, peace, and love. These good gifts are enjoyed precisely because God has given Christians the greatest gift of all: new life; regeneration and salvation through the power of the gospel.

James explains, "Of His own will He brought us forth by the word of truth, that we might be a kind of first fruits of His creatures." The greatest and most perfect gift that comes from above is the gift of new life.

Delight in the gospel

Of God's own will He "brought us forth by the word of truth." That is, He birthed us or "caused us to be born again by the word of truth," by the gospel.

Christians have been "brought forth" or birthed again by means of the gospel. And James adds that our being given new life does not end with us. God gives us new life "that we might be a kind of first fruits of His creatures."

The term "first fruits" is an agrarian term, a reference to the farmer's first gleanings, "first fruits" of the harvest. The first gleanings were a sign of a greater harvest to come. So we believers are "a kind of first fruits of His (God's) creatures," the first saved souls of more to come, the promise of more children with new natures to come, more persons who will be born again, more persons "brought forth by the word of truth," by the gospel.

So Christians successfully tackle temptation by delighting in the gospel. Of all the good and perfect gifts God has given, new life in Christ is unquestionably the best! In fact, apart from the gift of salvation, Christians cannot enjoy any of the other gifts such as true peace, love, and joy.

Delighting continuously in the goodness of God is the secret to tackling temptation. Intentional reflection upon the joy of our salvation is the means by which we will walk in holiness.

Earlier we recalled King David's sin with Bathsheba. Most of us know the story quite well. Sometime after David sinned, he was confronted by Nathan the prophet and repented.

We have Psalm 51 as one of David's greatest psalms of confession and repentance. It was written after David had been confronted by Nathan. One of the most stirring lines in the psalm is where David writes, "Restore to me the joy of Your salvation (verse 12)."

Have you ever wondered precisely when David lost his joy? Surely it did not happen all at once. It is hard to imagine David's suddenly losing all of his joy moments before, or even moments after, his noticing Bathsheba. Does it not stand to reason that David lost the joy of his salvation long before that infamous evening?

In a practical devotional, writer Timothy Paul Jones considers this very question:

> I would suggest that David's loss of joy was not the result of his sin but part of the cause. David's sinful actions were the fruit of his failure to recall that the lasting joy of God's salvation far outstripped the passing pleasure of Bathsheba's flesh. David had already lost sight of the joy of God's salvation before he saw the young woman bathing on the roof and chose to call her into his chambers. It was, at least in part, due to David's misplaced joy that he sacrificed his integrity for a false and fleeting joy that could never satisfy his soul. Now, the penitent king begged God to restore his lost joy.

Then Jones pens these memorable words:

37

"Purity flows from a heart that recognizes the joy of God's salvation as a gift more satisfying than any competing pleasure the world can provide."[7]

Christians must say "No" to that which is bad by saying "Yes" to that which is good. If we are walking regularly with the Lord, daily finding our soul's satisfaction in Christ, delighting in God's goodness and God's gospel, then we are more likely to prevail over temptation. We will battle temptation from a position of strength rather than a position of weakness.

What About You?

"You can't keep birds from flying over your head, but you can keep them from building a nest in your hair." What are some of the "birds" that pester you? How can you "keep them from building a nest in your hair?"

Paul writes that when Christians are tempted, God has made "the way of escape" for them (1 Corinthians 10:13)." What exactly is "the way of escape" and how does it work?

Are you honestly experiencing "the joy of God's salvation?" If so, how can you sustain that joy? If not, what can you do to get it—or get it back?

Chapter 5: A Check-up from the Neck up
(James 1:19-21)

19 So then, my beloved brethren, let every man be swift to hear, slow to speak, slow to wrath;
20 for the wrath of man does not produce the righteousness of God.
21 Therefore lay aside all filthiness and overflow of wickedness, and receive with meekness the implanted word, which is able to save your souls.

In the previous chapter we learned that one key to enduring trials and avoiding temptation is to delight in God's goodness and to delight in the gospel. James now turns to some practical expressions of our living out the gospel. Remember that this letter is written to Christians. James is not writing here about *becoming* a Christian, he's writing about *behaving* as a Christian.

The phrase at the beginning of this passage seems to build upon this gospel foundation. James writes, "So then," which is better translated, "So know this," or "Take note of this." We might say, "Listen up!" And then James goes on to call for practical Christian evidences that flow from a changed life.

Particularly in view here are Christian behaviors related to speaking, hearing, and thinking. Given this area of focus, you could say James is asking us to participate in a "Check-up from the neck up."

Watch Your Mouth

James instructs first: "Let every man be swift to hear" and "slow to speak." In the words used by many of our mothers: Watch your mouth! There are two important actions regarding proper use of our mouths: we must close them tightly when we listen, and open them slowly when we speak.

Close tightly when you listen

Be a good listener. Don't become the person you yourself recognize as a bad listener. We all know the type. You're talking to this person and all the while you get the sense that this person isn't really listening, but is rather thinking of what they're going to say when you are finished. And you feel like you need to hurry through the rest of your words in order to make a point because they're getting ready to interrupt you to speak their mind. Don't do that!

Exercise restraint and keep your mouth closed while you listen to whoever is talking to you. Honor them by looking them in the eye and taking time to hear them out. Listen. Then, when it is your turn to speak, take care to speak wisely.

Open slowly when you speak

Someone said God has given us two ears and one mouth so we would listen twice as much as we would speak. Be a good listener. Know the danger of talking too much, of being a chatterbox.

Solomon warns, " When words are many, sin is not absent, but he who holds his tongue is wise (Proverbs 10:19)." In another place he advises, "Even a fool is thought wise if he keeps silent, and discerning if he holds his tongue (Proverbs 17:28)."

Are you a good listener? Here's a helpful question: What do you do with your cell phone when someone is talking to you? Let me suggest you put it away. Put it in your pocket or in your purse. Silence it. Honor the person who is talking to you by giving your full attention. When you turn to your phone to look at a text or a tweet or whatever, you are dishonoring the person who is talking to you and turning to someone else who is actually interrupting and doesn't know it. Exercise the wisdom of restraint. Be swift to hear.

James moves from the discipline of proper speaking and hearing to the discipline of proper thinking, especially the thinking we do in response to emotions.

Keep Your Head

Our initial response to jarring emotions is often wrong. We may allow our emotions to get the best of us and fail to "keep our head" as Rudyard Kipling advises in his famous poem "If —" which begins with a call to "keep your head when all about you are losing theirs and blaming it on you."

Keep your head. In other words, don't react in a way you will later regret. Paul writes, "Be angry and do not sin (Ephesians 4:26)." Don't allow your anger to lead you down a path that will hurt others and bring shame upon the Lord. Rather, James says, be "slow to wrath."

Be calm

To be "slow to wrath" is to be calm, unruffled, and even-tempered. Apply this to the context of James' call for wise listening and speaking. If we respond rashly to a criticism or concern, we may sin by saying or doing something we later regret. We may even lash out in response, endeavoring to project our wrong onto others.

41

Hear again the wisdom of Solomon: "A gentle answer turns away wrath, but a harsh word stirs up anger (Proverbs 15:1)."

Watch your mouth. Keep your head. They go together. "Let every man be swift to hear, slow to speak, slow to wrath."

A lady once approached evangelist Billy Sunday in an effort to defend her frequent angry outbursts. She reasoned, "There is nothing wrong with losing my temper," adding, "I just quickly blow up, and then it's all over." Sunday wisely responded, "So does a shotgun. It quickly blows up, and look at the damage it leaves behind."

It is nearly always better to be in the position of wishing you *had* said something than to be in the position of regretting what you *actually said*. How often do we wish we had not said what we actually said to our son, daughter, parents, or spouse? Indeed, "when words are many, sin is not absent, but he who holds his tongue is wise (Proverbs 10:19)."

Be Christlike

James goes on to say why being an angry and bitter person is so unbecoming of a Christian. He argues, "for the wrath of man does not produce the righteousness of God."

When James uses the word "righteousness" in his letter, the meaning is generally different from the way Paul uses the same word in his letters. James is not talking about "saving righteousness" or, "imputed righteousness," the righteousness of Christ. He does not have the doctrine of justification in mind. Again, his letter is not about *becoming* a Christian, but about *behaving* as a Christian.

When James uses the word "righteousness" in his letter, he generally has in view the practical expression of one's faith, the daily behavior of believers, actions that are consistent with their faith.

It's the same understanding of righteousness Jesus taught in the Sermon on the Mount. He said, for example:

> Be careful not to practice your righteousness in front of others to be seen by them…So when you give to the needy, do not announce it with trumpets, as the hypocrites do in the synagogues and on the streets, to be honored by others (Matthew 6:1-2; NIV)."

So James warns: "the wrath of man does not produce the righteousness of God." A paraphrase of this verse may be: "When you lash out at someone, allowing your anger to get the best of you, you do not look like a follower of Jesus. Your behavior is inconsistent with the faith you profess. This does not please God!"

Hear from God

In an effort to correct the inconsistent actions of Christians who allow their emotions to get the better of them, James turns to helpful correction, correction culminating in our receiving the Word of God, or hearing from God. There are two necessary actions for believers to be in a position to hear from God: rejecting and receiving.

Reject all wicked activity

James admonishes: "Therefore lay aside all filthiness and overflow of wickedness." The "laying aside" of all wickedness conveys the action of removing things that are undesirable, things that don't look right on us, things that don't "suit" us, much the way dirty clothes don't look right on us. So what do we do? We take off the dirty clothes, laying them aside, putting on clean clothes. Applied to Christian living, the dirty clothes are the ways we used to live before we became Christians. Now that we are Christians, we live differently and look differently. We are spiritually clean so we endeavor to look that way and live that way. We will not put on our old, dirty clothes of old behavior any longer, because we are now different.

It's the same idea conveyed by the Apostle Paul: "Let us cast off the works of darkness, and let us put on the armor of light (Romans 13:12; *cf.* Colossians 3:5-14)."

James describes that old behavior, that pre-conversion behavior, as "all filthiness and overflow of wickedness." He suggests we must "lay aside" these dirty ways of thinking and living in order to be in a proper position to "receive" the Word, to hear from God—much like the way we need to clean out our ears so we can hear properly.

Consider how anger and wrath can impede your ability to hear the Word. If you have anger and bitterness in your spirit, it's really hard to listen to preaching or teaching of the Word. I know that from my own experience. To hear from God, we must reject all wicked activity.

Receive the word in humility

Having described what we must *reject*, James turns next to what we must *receive*: "receive with meekness the implanted word, which is able to save your souls."

The "implanted word" is God's Word, namely what God says as recorded in Scripture. This is the Word "which is able to save your souls," and James most likely uses the word "save" here in a general sense as in, "saving you from a lot of trouble," because he is addressing professing Christians, folks who are already saved. At the same time, however, the Word of God is certainly that Word which is able to save *all* souls! The Word of God contains the saving message of the gospel and all who believe and receive the gospel message may be saved.

Yet James' main concern here is *how* one receives the Word of God. He writes: "Receive *with meekness* the implanted word." The word meekness connotes humility, a teachable spirit. Receive the Word by listening sincerely, assuming the posture of a teachable spirit.

Do you have a teachable spirit? Do you receive the Word of God with anticipation? Consider how you arrive for public worship where the Word is preached or a small group setting where the Word is taught. Do you hunger for preaching and teaching of the Word? Do you thirst for it because you really want to learn and grow? Or does your body language and general disposition suggest you've pretty well learned all you care to learn?

James says, "Receive with meekness (with humility) the implanted Word, which is able to save your souls." Have a teachable spirit. Demonstrate a willingness to hear, to listen, to learn.

And James refers to the Word as that which is "implanted" in the Christian. When the Christian reads or hears the Word, the Word is planted within. To borrow from Jesus' parable, the Word is sown in the heart just as a farmer's seed is sown in the ground (Luke 8:4-15). The Christian must receive the Word with a fertile attitude if he is to benefit from it. Whether the implanted Word ripens to a harvest depends upon the receptivity, the meekness, of the one receiving it.

True believers have a natural thirst and hunger for the Word of God. Because believers have been "born again," they have new natures with new desires. Their soul yearns for the food that results in spiritual growth. That food is God's Word.

Before a person is saved, the Word is not that important to him. He may find it occasionally helpful or interesting. After all, a person doesn't need to be a Christian in order to find the Bible interesting. A lost person, a non-Christian, may find sections of the Bible rather engaging, even useful at times.

But one of the ways a person knows he is born again is that the Bible is more to him than merely an interesting or helpful book; it is food for the soul! The Christian has an inherent love for the

Word of God and feels he or she must have it, must read it, must hear it, or there will be no growth, no power, and no life.

Imagine you have been marooned on and island and haven't eaten for several weeks and you are famished. After your rescue you are seated at a table where there's a roast and potatoes and gravy. How will you respond? Will you think to yourself, "Well, this all looks rather interesting. I suppose if I eat some of this it will even be helpful?" No, you are hungry! You have natural desires within causing you to crave that meat and you are going to take in as much as you can with great delight.

One reason many professing Christians may lose their joy of feasting upon the Word is because they are trying to satisfy their spiritual hunger pangs with the wrong "food." There is so much "junk food" in our culture, so much "filthiness and overflow of wickedness" that we may be receiving this "food" perhaps without our even realizing it.

In the same way, a person may gorge himself on unhealthy food, depriving his body of necessary nutrients. The Christian may unwittingly fill himself with the unhealthy food of contemporary culture, causing his spiritual body to languish and weaken.

Think of all the "noise" in our culture that prevents us from hearing the Word: there is ungodly conversation, ungodly music, ungodly books, magazines, and websites. There are ungodly movies, sitcoms, and Broadway productions. I realize there are those who defend Christian participation in some of these activities. My point is that there is so much unhelpful "noise" blasting into our lives that we must take care not to allow the Word of God to be silenced. To the Christian, God's Word is naturally "music" to his ears. It is beautiful. It is wholesome. It is healthy. It is life.

So it is not enough merely to "plug our ears," silencing the noise. As we've noted before, we must not only say "No" to something, we must also say "Yes" to something else. We must reject that which is bad and receive that which is good.

In the Greek mythological epic, *The Argonautica*, there is a memorable scene where the legendary musician Orpheus helps his sailing companions overcome the beguiling music of the Sirens. These are the same Sirens Odysseus encounters in Homer's *The Odyssey* where Odysseus puts wax into the sailers' ears so that they would not be enchanted by the music and thus drawn inexorably to certain death. In *The Argonautica,* Orpheus plays masterfully upon his lyre, drowning out the seducing sounds of the Sirens so that the Argo sailers may pass by safely.

The bewitching music of the Sirens is much like the noise of the world. Christians must take care to say "No" to that which is unhelpful and dangerous. At the same time, however, they must also say "Yes" to that which is helpful and life-giving: the Word of God. We must listen to the beautiful music of God's Word, receiving with meekness the Word that is able to save our souls.[8]

What About You?

Do you have a natural hunger for the Word of God? If not, why do you think that is?

How might you best prepare to "hear" the Word in corporate worship? In Bible study?

What is some of the "noise" in your life that competes with your hearing from God?

Chapter 6: Be Doers of the Word
(James 1:22-25)

22 But be doers of the word, and not hearers only, deceiving yourselves.
23 For if anyone is a hearer of the word and not a doer, he is like a man observing his natural face in a mirror;
24 for he observes himself, goes away, and immediately forgets what kind of man he was.
25 But he who looks into the perfect law of liberty and continues in it, and is not a forgetful hearer but a doer of the work, this one will be blessed in what he does.

S uppose you give a friend a cookbook. It's full of wonderful recipes and contains everything necessary to guide him through the steps of preparing a number of delightful dishes. You check back with your friend six months later and ask how he likes the cookbook. He says, "Oh, I love it!" You respond, "Great! What are some of the meals you have enjoyed?" He says, "I haven't enjoyed any." You reply, "But I thought you said you loved the cookbook?" He says, "Yes, I love it very much! I have marked all through it. I have underlined some of my favorite places. I've highlighted certain sections and even earmarked a few pages I especially enjoyed. I even got it signed on the inside cover by a renowned chef." Perplexed you ask, "But while you have marked throughout the book these several months, you mean to say that you have never actually prepared a single meal? You've never actually *done* what it says?!" And your friend replies, "Right, but I sure love reading it!"

I suppose that imaginary scenario seems rather unlikely, but many Christians treat the Bible much the way our friend treated his cookbook. Some Christians say, "Oh, the Bible blesses me so much! I've underlined some of my favorite verses. I've written in the margins and highlighted different sections with different colored pens." Some may even boast of having had a particular evangelist sign the inside cover.

Given what James teaches in the verses above, we may imagine his responding rather tersely to such Christians: "Look, I'm glad you love the word of God. There's nothing wrong with underlining and highlighting. But be sure you are not only a *hearer*, but a *doer* of the Word. Do what it says!"

Correctly Respond to it

Everyone responds to the Word in some way or other. James is telling us to respond to the Word correctly. An incorrect response would be merely to hear the Word and do nothing with it. But James says, "be doers of the word, and not hearers only, deceiving yourselves."

That word "deceiving" is a term that means to make a miscalculation. A person who reasons that he has done his duty merely by being present in a worship service, listening to the wonderful music, and enjoying the minister's message is, according to James, making a miscalculation. He is deceiving himself.

The New Living Translation puts it this way: "Don't just listen to God's word. You must do what it says. Otherwise, you are only fooling yourselves."

Imagine a medical patient receiving instructions for how to beat a debilitating disease. The doctor says, "You know, what you have may prove fatal, but there is hope. Here is what you need to do: take this medicine, follow this regimen, and you will be well." If the patient reasons that has done enough merely by listening to the doctor's instructions, then that patient has made a serious miscalculation!

Christians must "receive with meekness the implanted word which is able to save their souls (James 1:21)." Christians must both hear and do what the Bible says. In fact, *all* persons must hear and do what the Bible says, Christians and non-Christians alike.

Herod was not a believer. Interestingly, he enjoyed hearing John the Baptist's preaching. The Bible says Herod "heard him gladly (Mark 6:20)," but he didn't do what John preached. He remained an unbeliever. Ironically, he would eventually order the beheading of John the Baptist—the very one whose message he had enjoyed hearing! John had preached a message of repentance and Herod never repented. To use James' words: Herod was merely a *hearer*, but not a *doer* of the Word.

There are many persons, no doubt, who believe they are going to heaven merely because they have heard biblical teaching. They have attended worship, they have heard the gospel. Perhaps they have even enjoyed themselves in the process. But it is not enough simply to hear the gospel; one must correctly respond to the gospel. One must confess his sin, repent, and believe that Jesus Christ is the only Savior through whom forgiveness comes (Luke 5:31-32; John 3:36; John 14:6; Acts 3:19; Acts 20:21; 1 Timothy 2:5).

If anyone would be certain of his salvation, he must not only hear what the Word teaches, he must do what it says. He must correctly respond to it. There is something else here that James teaches about the Word:

Carefully Reflect on it

James provides a very useful illustration. We are to imagine a man who has heard the Word but does not do what it says. James writes: "He is like a man observing his natural face in a mirror; for he observes himself, goes away, and immediately forgets what kind of man he was."

When James wrote this letter over two thousand years ago, there were no glass mirrors like those we enjoy today. Mirrors in the time of the New Testament were a polished metal of some kind, polished silver, copper, or tin. They were, however, a sufficient means by which to see one's image.

As I grow older, I find that looking in the mirror sometimes makes me wince. A mirror is honest. It's not like taking a picture of yourself where you can edit the picture and choose from a number of filters that soften the edges, add hair, or smooth out the lines. A mirror is honest. You can't "Photoshop" that reflection!

So I look into the mirror and see things that need correction, like where I need to cut back on the food, or exercise more. It's not the mirror that needs correction, it's what I see in the mirror that needs to be fixed.

When we read the Bible, we may not immediately like what we see. The problem, however, is not the Bible. The problem is what we learn about ourselves when we read the Bible. Truth calls for change and change is often difficult. At the same time, if we will allow the Bible to address our behavior and then respond correctly after careful reflection—not just hearing but doing what it says—we absolutely will be the better for it.

Describing the Bible as "the perfect law of liberty," James writes: "He who looks into the perfect law of liberty and continues in it, and is not a forgetful hearer but a doer of the work, this one will be blessed in what he does." So blessing comes when we are "not a forgetful hearer" but a doer of what we read. We continue to read and remember the Word.

Continually Read & Remember it

The word "looks" is in the active voice and conveys the idea of continual action, looking intently, endeavoring to get a good, thorough look. It is "to stoop down and look into." It's the same word used in John's Gospel where John writes about his visiting the empty tomb of Jesus and stooping down and looking into the tomb (John 20:5).

So James says that if we "look into the perfect law of liberty (the Word which sets us free)," and we don't forget what we read, but actually do what it says, then we will be blessed in what we do.

How easy it is to be a "forgetful hearer!" You can hear the Word in worship or in Bible study and then walk out of the classroom or out of the sanctuary, immediately forgetting what you've heard. Too often conversation centers upon sports, the weather, or what we're going to eat.

Unless we are disciplined to remember what we have read—by reflecting upon it and then putting it into action—we will be a "forgetful hearer."

For example, if you have recently read that Jesus says, "Love your enemies," then don't forget it when someone hurts you this week. If you have read where Paul says, "Forgive as you've been forgiven," then remember that when a loved one breaks your heart. Perhaps you have read recently that the Bible says, "God loves a cheerful giver," then remember that the next time you write out a check.

Of course we are more likely to remember biblical teaching when we spend time reading the Bible.

Here's a practical question: Do you believe everything you see on television? Or on the internet? Or in the newspaper? My guess is that you would answer in the negative.

On the other hand, what if I asked, "Do you believe everything you read in the Bible?" Most evangelicals would answer in the positive: "Yes! I absolutely believe everything I read in the Bible."

If so, here is the follow-up question: "Do you spend more time reading things you *don't* believe, or reading things you *do* believe?"

It's a fair question, isn't it? Many of us really believe the Bible to be absolutely trustworthy in all that it teaches. We believe the Bible to be inerrant, totally free from error and incapable of ever being disproven. Yet, how much time do we actually spend reading from this powerful book, especially given the time we spend reading other books or sitting in front of screens?

Reading the Bible is one of the main ways we are able to grow and have a meaningful relationship with God, the ultimate author of the Bible. Think of it: the Bible is the only book whose author is with us every time we read it!

We grow in our Christian walk by letting God speak to us. That means we allow him to correct us as well as encourage us. Just as a marriage thrives when each spouse has the freedom to communicate everything—the good, the bad, and the ugly—so our relationship with God thrives when we allow Him to share everything with us. If we only read certain parts of the Bible and skip over difficult passages, we are like a controlling spouse who "shuts down" the one he loves when hearing the truth becomes too painful. Our relationship with God matures and deepens, however, when we allow God to address us in our sin.

Allow the Bible to speak to you! Allow the Bible to "call you out" on your behavior. Then correct that errant behavior by doing what the Bible says. If you do this, James promises we will be blessed in return.

We've noted before that James frequently echoes the teachings of his half-brother Jesus. Jesus talks about being a "doer" of the Word and not merely a "hearer." Listen to the way He concludes the famous, "Sermon on the Mount."

> "Therefore whoever hears these sayings of Mine, and does them, I will liken him to a wise man who built his house on the rock: and the rain descended, the floods came, and the winds blew and beat on that house; and it did not fall, for it was founded on the rock. But everyone who hears these sayings of Mine, and does not do them, will be like a foolish man who built his house on the sand: and the rain descended, the floods came, and the winds blew and beat on that house; and it fell. And great was its fall." (Matthew 7:24-27).

Don't be a forgetful hearer of the Word. Do what it says!

What About You?

Are there places in the Bible you'd rather not read because they address behaviors you are unwilling to change?

Why do you think James refers to the Bible as "the perfect law of liberty?"

What can you do this week to keep from becoming a "forgetful hearer" of the Word?

Chapter 7: When Religion is Useless
(James 1:26-27)

26 If anyone among you thinks he is religious, and does not bridle his tongue but deceives his own heart, this one's religion is useless.
27 Pure and undefiled religion before God and the Father is this: to visit orphans and widows in their trouble, and to keep oneself unspotted from the world.

H aving taught in the previous chapter about being a "doer" of the Word, James now provides practical examples of what "doing" the Word looks like.

Immediately evident in these two verses is the occurrence of the word "religious" or "religion." It occurs three times. This fact reminds us that the word "religion" is not a bad word, it is a Bible word.

I mention this because many evangelicals resist using this word. We are known for saying frequently that we are not interested in a "religion, but a relationship," meaning of course, a relationship with Jesus. After all, Christianity is not a man-centered works-based, self-improvement system of religious rules and regulations. It is rather a relationship with Jesus Christ. As someone has said, "the world has many religions, but only one gospel."

Given James' audience, however, we can appreciate his use of the word "religion." We have frequently noted that James is writing not so much about *becoming* a Christian as he is about *behaving* as a Christian. So when James uses the terms "religion" or "religious," he is talking about a Christian faith that is lived-out through practical expression (*cf.* James 2:1, 14).

If Christian faith is not lived-out through practical expression, through "doing" what we "hear," then James concludes our religion is "useless." If we wish to keep our religion from becoming useless, then we had better behave in the three ways James discusses in these verses.

Godly Conversation

Having already introduced the need for control over our tongues (James 1:19), James now provides another "appetizer" before laying down his "full course" presentation on the tongue (James 3:1-12). He writes, "If anyone among you thinks he is religious, and does not bridle his tongue," then he is one who "deceives his own heart" and his religion is "useless."

To "bridle" one's tongue conjures up images of bridling a horse. A bridle is a headgear placed on a horse in an effort to control the movement of the horse. Similarly, Christians must bridle their tongues in an effort to control the movement of their words.

In fact, James asserts that if Christians choose *not* to bridle their tongues, then they are "deceiving their own hearts" and their religion is useless. Put another way: You can't expect to be considered a true Christian if you don't exercise control over the words you speak. Christians are to be known for wholesome, helpful speech.

The Apostle Paul agrees. He writes, "Let no corrupt word proceed out of your mouth, but what is good for necessary edification, that it may impart grace to the hearers (Ephesians 4:29)" and, "Let your speech always be with grace, seasoned with salt, that you may know how you ought to answer each one (Colossians 4:6)."

The call for "bridling our tongues" suggests that we have a natural, fallen tendency to allow our tongues to go *unbridled*." Too often we fail to exercise restraint over our speech. We speak before thinking and allow our tongues to get us into all kinds of trouble.

I love the little poem by an unknown author, the rhyme entitled "Our Lips and Ears."

If you your lips would keep from slips,
Five things observe with care:
Of whom you speak, to whom you speak,
And how and when and where.

If you your ears would save from jeers,
These things keep meekly hid:
Myself and I, and mine and my,
And how I do and did.

If we don't take care to bridle our tongues, we may find ourselves engaged in unhelpful and unhealthy conversations—boastings, gossip, and slander to name just a few.

Jesus teaches that a man's speech is a reflection of what is in his heart. He says, "Those things which proceed out of the mouth come from the heart and they defile a man. For out of the heart proceed evil thoughts, murders, adulteries, fornications, thefts, false witness, blasphemies (Matthew 15:18-19)."

How careful we must be to "bridle our tongues!" May the Lord grant us the grace of restraining our tongues so that we may engage only in godly conversation.

Godly Concern

James next calls upon Christians to show love and mercy toward those who were often overlooked in the church: orphans and widows. He says true faith in Christ will result in visiting these dear people.

James' use of the word "visit" connotes more than just a physical visit or dropping by. It means "to look after" and "to care for," which would include visiting, but suggests more the idea of showing practical concern and compassion for those who are less fortunate.

In New Testament times, widowed women were especially vulnerable to poverty and neglect. In his first letter to Timothy, the Apostle Paul wrote that the immediate family had the initial responsibility of caring for widowed mothers and grandmothers. If there were no immediate family, however, the church was instructed to make a list of those who were widows to ensure that they received adequate ministry (1 Timothy 5:3-16).

The New Testament office of deacon ("one who serves"), is a ministry that arose out of the need to care for neglected widows (Acts 6:1-7).

Orphans were another example of those who were easily neglected in biblical times. If the father of a family died, his wife and children were suddenly without financial resources, often indebted to lenders, with little opportunity to immediately rectify the situation.

Widows and orphans face similar challenges today, especially in third world countries and similar places where poverty is common and opportunity is scarce.

While our country has a number of good public and private social programs to care for widows and orphans, the primary responsibility for their care rests with the local church, especially where those widows and orphans are connected to the congregation.

One reason many Christians and churches are involved in crisis pregnancy resource centers is precisely because of the "orphaned state" of the unborn. An unborn child's life is at risk when its parents feel they are unable to care for it.

Of all people Christians in particular must show a godly concern for others, promoting the sanctity of life and human flourishing. In addition to intentional involvement in right-to-life ministries, many Christians recognize the benefit of adopting children, providing care and spiritual support for those children who otherwise would be unlikely to receive it.

If we are to keep our religion from becoming useless, we must have godly conversation and godly concern. But there is something else here: James also provides a succinct statement regarding the Christian's personal holiness.

Godly Conduct

James says that Christians must keep themselves "unspotted from the world."

It's a helpful visual: "To keep oneself unspotted from the world" pictures a man or woman with a spot on himself or herself; a man or woman who is corrupted by worldly influences.

Later in Chapter 4, James will speak more directly to this challenge. He will ask, "Do you not know that friendship with the world is enmity with God? Whoever therefore wants to be a friend of the world makes himself an enemy of God (James 4:4)."

Many professing Christians think far too little of their engaging in worldly behaviors. The enemy seeks to ensnare believers in gossip, sexual impurity, pornography, or joking about ungodly things.

Anytime we engage in ungodly behavior—if even just for a moment—we are in jeopardy of losing our Christian influence. People are not won over to our faith in Christ when we say one thing with our testimony and we say another thing altogether by our actions.

A few years ago there was a popular advertisement for a laundry detergent stick. One of the TV commercials showed a guy with a spot on his shirt. And the guy is interviewing for a job and he is trying to talk, but all the while the little spot on his shirt is drawing attention to itself. Every time the guy tries to talk during the interview, the little stain on his shirt is talking at the same time. It's going, "Blah, blah, blah," so that the interviewer can't hear what the interviewee is saying. The spot overpowers him! The commercial ends with a picture of the detergent stick and the words: "Silence the stain instantly."

The whole point of the commercial is that people can't really hear what we're saying if we have a spot that diverts their attention away from our message. In the same way, you and I can never hope to point people to Jesus when we have allowed ourselves to be spotted by the world. The spots of worldliness in our conduct speak louder than the words of our Christian testimony. We must "silence the stain" by confessing our sin, repenting from it, and endeavoring to walk in moral purity. We must have godly conduct.

What About You?

Given James' uses of the term, how do you feel about using the word "religion" to describe your Christian faith?

What does your church do to show concern for widows and orphans?

Are there any behaviors in your life that may be silencing your verbal witness? If so, what will you do this week to change your behavior?

✳ ✳ ✳

Chapter 8: The Sin of Showing Favoritism

(James 2:1-7)

1 My brethren, do not hold the faith of our Lord Jesus Christ, the Lord of glory, with partiality.
2 For if there should come into your assembly a man with gold rings, in fine apparel, and there should also come in a poor man in filthy clothes,
3 and you pay attention to the one wearing the fine clothes and say to him, "You sit here in a good place," and say to the poor man, "You stand there," or, "Sit here at my footstool,"
4 have you not shown partiality among yourselves, and become judges with evil thoughts?
5 Listen, my beloved brethren: Has God not chosen the poor of this world to be rich in faith and heirs of the kingdom which He promised to those who love Him?
6 But you have dishonored the poor man. Do not the rich oppress you and drag you into the courts?
7 Do they not blaspheme that noble name by which you are called?

Second only to Jesus, James is arguably the master of vivid illustrations. In this passage he paints a picture easily imagined by regular worship attenders. Two people from two different backgrounds enter into the gathered assembly. Those in a position to welcome these two persons will be tempted to treat them differently based upon appearance alone. James calls this behavior a sin (verse 9) and warns the church against it.

Favoritism is Incompatible with Faith

James says that Christians must not hold their faith in Christ "with partiality." This word "partiality" is in a plural form so it could be translated as "favoritisms." In other words, there is more than one way to show favoritism. James addresses primarily the matter of showing favoritism to those who appear especially wealthy, but that is just one illustration of favoritism. We may play favorites with respect to those who are more attractive than others, more powerful than others, or more influential than others.

We may discriminate against others on the basis of education, gender, race, or ethnicity. Again, there is more than one way to show partiality or favoritism.

One of the reasons favoritism is incompatible with faith in Christ is because drawing attention to a special characteristic or status of others is, in essence, ascribing a kind of glory to them. The word "glory" carries the notion of weight and worth. So when we show favoritism to certain people we are saying, "This person carries a lot of weight" or, "This person has clout; this person is really influential."

Yet note how James identifies our Lord Jesus. He describes Him as "the Lord of glory." Literally the Greek reads "Jesus Christ, the glory." Favoritism is incompatible with your faith in Jesus Christ, *the* glory.

Jesus Christ is the glory of God. Man is *not* the glory. God is the glory and He will not trade His glory with another (Isaiah 42:8). Paul says in 1 Corinthians 1:15 that Christ is "the image of the invisible God, the firstborn over all creation." And the writer of Hebrews declares that Jesus Christ is "the brightness of [God's] glory and the express image of His person (Hebrews 1:3)."

Showing favoritism to another person, then, is a way of ascribing glory to another when all glory belongs to God. Favoritism is incompatible with faith. But how easily a spirit of favoritism can creep into the church!

Favoritism can Infect the Fellowship

This is James' concern here as he describes the aforementioned illustration of two different visitors entering the church building: "a man with gold rings, in fine apparel" and another person described as "a poor man in filthy clothes."

Stop for a moment and consider your own immediate inclination. Were you in a position to welcome these two visitors, who would you be more likely to approach first? Be honest! Would you be more likely to greet the man richly attired who is presumably also personable and influential? Or would you be more likely to reach out to the shabbily dressed man? Each must answer for himself, but James seems to suggest that most of us would treat the rich man more graciously than we would the poor man.

Favoritism occurs when we focus merely upon the externals. In a memorable verse, the Lord told the Prophet Samuel: "Man looks on the outward appearance, but God looks on the heart (1 Samuel 16:7)."

Of course James is not saying that it is wrong to *honor* others. It is certainly appropriate to give up a seat to honor someone, an elderly person, a special visiting friend, or a military serviceman, for example.

In some cultures, ministers are honored with front seats in worship assemblies. I recall the first time I witnessed this on a mission trip in South America. Perfectly happy to sit comfortably in the back or midway among the pews, our host insisted that I sit right up front. He even moved women and children out of the way to make room. I remember feeling awkward and cringing as I tried in vain to refuse the honor. But the host insisted —as did the women and children! They were delighted to honor me with a special seat up front.

Honoring others in this fashion is not what James has in mind. James is talking about our wrongly esteeming others merely on the basis of physical appearance. In the illustration provided, no one deserves special treatment on the basis of his wealth.

William Barclay helps us imagine this "man with gold rings" who visits the assembly. He writes:

> The more ostentatious of the ancients wore rings on every finger except the middle one, and wore far more than one on each finger. They even hired rings to wear when they wished to give an impression of special wealth. "We adorn our fingers with rings," said Seneca, "and we distribute gems over every joint."[9]

So let's imaginatively personalize James' illustration in the context of the contemporary church. Here's this guy, we'll call him "Mr. Bling," and he's probably married to "Mrs. Bedazzle." So Mr. Bling comes into the sanctuary and the ushers are tripping over themselves to get to him. They're like "Hey, I'll seat you right up front in the special seating." But to the poor guy they say reproachfully: "You, sit over there!" Or, "I'll tell you what: why don't you just sit right here next to my feet. I need a footstool and if my feet fall off the stool, you can put them back up for me."

This behavior seems unimaginable to many Christians, yet

James pushes us to consider our biases and prejudices.

When the rich young ruler approached Jesus, Jesus was not impressed with the man's externals. In fact, Jesus instructed the religious seeker to go and sell all that he had if he truly wished to follow Him (Luke 18:18-23). Jesus let the man, described by Luke as "very rich," walk away. I can't help but imagine that Jesus' disciples were beside themselves: "Jesus! That man has all kinds of money! What great influence we would have if he were part of our group!"

This is the sort of thinking we must be vigilant to guard against. There is no place for favoritism in the church. It is incompatible with the faith and we must not allow it to infect the fellowship. There is yet another main concern in the passage:

Favoritism is an Insult to the Family

James uses a term of endearment when addressing the church. He refers to them as "My dear brethren." He has in mind the entire church family, brothers and sisters (*cf*. James 2:2, 5, 14). The phrase "My dear brethren" is a reminder that Christians belong to a greater family, Christian brothers and sisters who love one another and will be there for one another in good times and bad.

The majority of Christians in James' day were poor (though cf James 5:1-6). So James is teaching that the church is dishonoring their own family by showing favoritism to the rich. After all it is the rich, James declares, "who oppress you and drag you into the courts." James is talking about rich *unbelievers* here. It is the rich non-Christians who were taking believers to court, needlessly litigating against them in an effort to exploit them. The actions of the rich were an insult to God. As James asks rhetorically, "Do they not blaspheme that noble name by which you are called?" The "noble name" is the name of Christ, the name by which Christians are known.

So when Christians were showing favoritism to the rich they

were, in essence, aligning themselves with those who were generally known for slandering Christ. James is not saying that it is wrong for Christians to be wealthy. He is simply pointing out that it was generally the wealthy of his day who were on the wrong side of the Christian faith. It's as if he were asking, "Why would you rather be aligned with unbelievers who are known for bringing shame upon the name of Jesus?"

Before we explore further this problem of favoritism, let's conclude by thanking God for His adopting us into His family apart from our externals. He did not choose us to be part of His family because of anything that would impress others. In the words of the Apostle Paul to the church at Corinth:

> Brothers and sisters, think of what you were when you were called. Not many of you were wise by human standards; not many were influential; not many were of noble birth. But God chose the foolish things of the world to shame the wise; God chose the weak things of the world to shame the strong.
> God chose the lowly things of this world and the despised things—and the things that are not—to nullify the things that are,
> so that no one may boast before him (1 Corinthians 1:26-29).

Here is a reminder that Christians have nothing for which to boast before God! Imagine if God *did* choose us on the merits of our special status or worth. How many of us then would qualify as Christians? Consider this: What if God chose us merely based upon external appearances or abilities and we didn't have what was required: enough money, enough influence, the right gender, the right skin color? Who of us would be saved?

Thankfully, God did *not* choose us on the basis of externals. He chose us on the basis of the perfect work of His Son Jesus Christ. And though there is wonderful mystery in the doctrine of election, this much we know: "whoever believes in Him will not perish, but will have everlasting life (John 3:16)." No matter our influence, background, socioeconomic condition, ethnicity, or gender, we may repent and believe in Jesus Christ and be saved from our sins.

What About You?

Given that James calls favoritism a sin (James 2:9), how will you treat others this week in your neighborhood, workplace, or school?

Do you really think of fellow church members as brothers and sisters? Do you treat your spiritual family members the same way you treat physical family members? Or do you treat them differently?

Of Jesus Paul writes: "though He was rich, yet for your sakes He became poor, that you through His poverty might become rich (2 Corinthians 8:9)." What does Paul mean?

Chapter 9: Love and Lawbreaking
(James 2:8-13)

8 If you really fulfill the royal law according to the Scripture, "You shall love your neighbor as yourself," you do well;
9 but if you show partiality, you commit sin, and are convicted by the law as transgressors.
10 For whoever shall keep the whole law, and yet stumble in one point, he is guilty of all.
11 For He who said, "Do not commit adultery," also said, "Do not murder." Now if you do not commit adultery, but you do murder, you have become a transgressor of the law.
12 So speak and so do as those who will be judged by the law of liberty.
13 For judgment is without mercy to the one who has shown no mercy. Mercy triumphs over judgment.

J esus says there is a way that others will know unmistakably that we are Christians. He says in John's Gospel, "By this all will know that you are My disciples, if you have love for one another (John 13:35)." And that love for one another is a love that extends to all persons without exception; our neighbors, or friends, and even our enemies. He says, "Bless those who curse you, do good to those who hate you, and pray for those who spitefully use you and persecute you…for if you love [only] those who love you, what reward do you have, or what good is that (Matthew 5:43-47)?"

Love is the distinguishing mark of all true disciples of the Lord Jesus Christ. If a person truly has the love of Christ within, then that love will manifest itself outwardly through loving actions.

If a man is physically sick, for example, he has something wrong on the inside. He has a bad heart, a virus, or a disease of some kind. What is wrong on the inside shows on the outside: his breathing is erratic, his color is bad, his body is weak. And others look at him and say, "You don't look so good." But then he gets what is wrong on the inside fixed. He has surgery or receives treatment. The procedure is completed and he is better on the inside and so it shows on the outside. His breathing is normal, his body is strong, his color is good. Others say, "You look good!" When we are healthy on the inside it shows on the outside.

Spiritually, we enter into this world dead in trespasses and sin (Ephesians 2:1). You might say we have a spiritual "heart condition." Our hearts are evil. They are hard and stony. We need to get what's wrong on the inside fixed. For Christians, God has performed a procedure, a "heart surgery." The Bible says in Ezekiel 36 that God takes out our heart of stone and replaces it with a new heart, a heart of flesh, a heart that is not hardened and calloused, but a heart that is soft and responsive to the will and way of God.

And once we are fixed on the inside, it shows on the outside. Things are different now. There is a change, a change that affects the way we live and the way we love.

Love Others without Partiality

In these verses James continues to warn the church against

showing favoritism or "showing partiality (2:1, 9)." You'll recall from Chapter 2 that we wrongly show partiality when we favor those who are dressed well over those who are not.

We show partiality when we favor those who are popular over those who are unpopular. And we show it when we favor those who are educated over those who are uneducated, those who have over those who have not, and those who are rich over those who are poor. We show partiality if we favor those who live on the "right" side of town, drive a certain kind of vehicle, go to a certain kind of school, talk a certain kind of way, or have a certain kind of skin color we believe to be the "right" color. Partiality, or favoritism, takes many forms.

Building upon this teaching, James writes that we "do well" if we truly fulfill what he calls "the royal law" in Scripture, namely: "You shall love your neighbor as yourself." The word "royal" means that which "belongs to the king," or the law of the kingdom (*cf*. verse 5).

We serve our Lord, our King, Jesus Christ. After all, Jesus Himself taught us to love, teaching us to love our neighbor as ourselves. And James is quoting from the Old Testament, specifically Leviticus 19:18: "You shall not take vengeance, nor bear any grudge against the children of your people, but you shall love your neighbor as yourself: I am the Lord."

Jesus was once asked about the greatest commandment. Matthew's Gospel describes a certain Pharisee who approached Jesus and asked Him a question, testing Him. He said: "Teacher, which is the great commandment in the law?" Jesus replied:

You shall love the Lord your God with all your heart, with all your soul, and with all your mind.' This is the first and great commandment. And the second is like it: 'You shall love your neighbor as yourself.' On these two commandments hang all the Law and the Prophets (Matthew 22:34-40).

There was another Pharisee who wanted to "justify himself" so he asked Jesus to expand upon His teaching, namely this matter of loving one's neighbors. He asked Jesus, "And who *is* my neighbor?" And Jesus answered his question by telling the parable of the Good Samaritan teaching, in essence, that our neighbor is anyone with whom we may come in contact (Luke 10:25-37).

Jesus also taught us to love those especially difficult to love. He commands:

> Bless those who curse you, do good to those who hate you, and pray for those who spitefully use you and persecute you...for if you love [only] those who love you, what reward do you have, or what good is that (Matthew 5:43-47)?

If you are a Christian you have been changed on the inside and that change will show up on the outside. You *will* love others. And by God's grace you will even love your enemies. James' focus is primarily upon loving those who are easily overlooked, like the "poor man in filthy clothes (James 2:2)." And James minces no words here. He warns: "but if you show partiality, you commit sin, and are convicted by the law as transgressors."

Make no mistake: showing partiality, or favoritism, is a sin. We are to love all people, treating all equally, showing favoritism to no one. Love others without partiality. There's something else here that James says Christians must do:

Obey the Law in its Entirety

James says: "For whoever shall keep the whole law, and yet stumble in one point, he is guilty of all." Given the examples provided in these verses, it seems clear that James has in mind what we often describe as the "moral law" in the Old Testament. Much of the "cultic law," such as dietary laws or other laws of rite and ritual, are no longer binding upon believers today. But the "moral law" is timeless. Every culture has some sense of moral law woven into the fabric of their social code, even if that culture fails to understand that the essence of their law is rooted in the grace of God.

For Christians, the moral law is aptly summarized in the "Ten Commandments" located in Exodus 20 and Deuteronomy 5. This moral law is a cohesive unit to be obeyed in its entirety. We are not permitted to ignore any of it. James says we are to "keep the whole law."

This raises a necessary clarification. Remember that James is writing to Christians. We've stated numerously that this letter is not about how to *become* a Christian, but how to *behave* as a Christian. James is writing to those who have been saved by grace through faith in Jesus Christ. So James is not teaching here that the way one is saved is by keeping the Old Testament Law, keeping the 10 Commandments.

Many people believe this is what the Bible teaches. Many people wrongly think that Christianity is about following rules and regulations in order to gain God's approval. But Christianity is not so much about following *principles* as it is about following a *Person,* namely Jesus Christ. Jesus is the only one who obeyed perfectly "the whole" law so that we could be forgiven of our sin. Once we have trusted Jesus as our Lord and Savior, we live out the moral law in obedience to God not as a means by which to be saved—that has been accomplished already through faith in Jesus Christ—but as a means of glorifying God with our new hearts.

One of the primary functions of the Old Testament law is to convict unbelievers of sin, forever pointing out their inability to keep the law and pointing to the only one who perfectly has, Jesus Christ (*cf.* Romans 3:20; Galatians 3:21-24).

The Bible is a mirror. As we look into it, we must allow it to show us what we are before we can expect to do what it says. We can't really do what it says until we first see what we are. We must first see our sin before we can rightly see our Savior. Then we turn to Him, trusting Him as Lord. We are saved by grace through faith in Christ. Jesus lived for us and died for us. He kept the law perfectly and thus fulfilled the law on our behalf. He died, taking our punishment for breaking the law, and He rose from the dead so we could be declared righteous by faith in Him (Romans 4:25).

So if we have been saved through faith in Christ, then the law is now "lived out" in us, not to *gain* our *justification*, but to *grow* in our *sanctification*. Christians live the law not in an effort to *get* saved; Christians live the moral law because they *are* saved.

James teaches that Christians, then, should be living out this moral law, by "keeping" it, keeping "the whole law." Again, William Barclay is helpful. He notes the erroneous way many in James' day thought of the Law:

> The Jew was very apt to regard the law as a series of detached injunctions. To keep one was to gain credit; to break one was to incur debt. A man could add up the ones he kept and subtract the ones he broke and so emerge with a credit or a debit balance.[10]

This is exactly how many today regard the observance of biblical commands. They think if they keep a biblical command they will gain a credit, and when they break a biblical command they will incur a debt. They hope that they will have more credits than debts in the end and perhaps tip the scales of justice in their favor or gain greater acceptance with God.

But one reason it is impossible to be saved by keeping the law (Romans 3:20; Galatians 3:16) is precisely because it is a cohesive unit. A person must obey it in its *entirety*—and no person does that *consistently* and *perfectly*. To break one *single* command is to break *all* the law, just as a single crack in the glass affects an entire windshield.

If you hope to be saved by keeping the law, you would have to keep *all* of it *consistently* and *perfectly*.

Think about taking a test in school. Say there are 100 questions worth one point each and you miss 5; you get a 95%. That's an A by most calculations. But imagine if you took that test and there were 100 questions worth one point each and you missed only one and received an F. You would argue, "But I got 99 right, I missed only one!" The teacher replies, "Doesn't matter. This test is a "pass" or "fail" test and because you did not get *all* of the questions correct, you fail."

If you're hoping to keep the Old Testament law as a means of earning salvation, you need to know that God does not grade on a curve. You've got to keep the whole law in its entirety. Breaking any one of the laws is to break all of them. Breaking just one command makes one "a transgressor of the law."

Here's another way to think of it: Imagine you are rushing to catch a plane. You are hurrying through check-in, moving quickly through the security line, and now running to the gate so you can catch the plane. But when you finally reach that gate it does not matter whether you are just one minute late or ten minutes late, once that gate is closed you are not getting on that plane. It doesn't matter how close you got, you are not allowed to board that flight.

If you are not a Christian, it doesn't matter how closely you try to follow the 10 Commandments. It really doesn't matter how "close" you get, because you are not saved by keeping the law. Nobody keeps the law consistently and perfectly—nobody but Jesus. That's why He is the only way in.

From the standpoint of an unbeliever, "sin is sin" whether it is murder or adultery or lying. Just one sin will keep a person from getting though the "gate" into heaven. It doesn't matter if it's a so-called "big" sin or a so-called "little" sin. Just one is enough to keep anyone from entering heaven.

This raises the need for another important word of clarification. While the phrase "sin is sin" is rightly used when referring to an unbeliever's inability to earn forgiveness or his hoping somehow to gain entrance to heaven based on an accrued number of "credits," it is not always helpful to use this phrase.

We should use the phrase "sin is sin" with care. Not all sins are equal in the sense that not all are equally heinous, equally ugly, or equally reprehensible. You may be fired from a job for lying to a co-worker or for beating a co-worker, but which would you rather have to explain at your next job interview?

Would you rather your daughter be found guilty of driving too fast or for robbing a bank? To say, "sin is sin" is to fail to account for degrees of wickedness as well as degrees of punishment or consequence.

Some sins are more or less heinous, but all are equally deadly in terms of a lost person's hope of gaining some sense of favor before God, doing good works in the hopes of becoming more "savable."

The law is a cohesive unit. It is an interdependent whole. It is to be obeyed in its entirety. So the Christian lives the law not in order to gain justification, but to grow in sanctification. And James reminds Christians that they are not permitted to "cherry pick" which commands they like and leave off those they don't like.

So you can't say, "Well, I know murder is bad and I'm not going to do that," but then you ignore the commandment forbidding adultery by lusting in your heart, which makes you a lawbreaker (Matthew 5:27-28). More to James' point: it is wrong to think, "Well, adultery and murder, I've never done these things and I never will," but then you show favoritism by being kind to rich people and shunning poor people. You have become a lawbreaker.

Love others without partiality and obey the law in its entirety. There's one more action James calls for in these verses:

Live with a View to Eternity

James reminds Christians that there's a judgment to come. He says, "So speak and so do as those who will be judged by the law of liberty." Every Christian will be judged one day, judged by the One True God.

The Apostle Paul writes: "We must all appear before the judgment seat of Christ, that each one may receive the things done in the body, according to what he has done, whether good or bad."—(2 Corinthians 5:10; *cf.* 1 Corinthians 3:12-15; 1 Peter 1:17).

Christians will one day stand before the Lord at the judgment. Thankfully, Christians will *not* be judged as to their justification. Christians are not in danger of facing condemnation, but they will be judged concerning their sanctification. In other words, Christians will be judged based upon how they "lived out" their Christian faith. This is a judgment that results in reward—or loss of reward.

It is reassuring to know that the true Christian will never hear Jesus say, "Depart from Me, I never knew you (Matthew 7:21-23)." Yet, he *will* be judged on the basis of what he has said and what he has done. "So speak and so do as those who will be judged by the law of liberty."

Christians will give an account for every word spoken (*cf.* Matthew 12:36) and for every deed done, whether good or bad. And Christians will receive reward for what they have done well, or experience loss of reward for what they have done poorly.

James says, "So speak and so do as those who will be judged by the law of liberty," the law that brings freedom, freedom from the penalty of sin. So speak and so do as those who will be judged by the law of liberty. And he adds, "For judgment is without mercy to the one who has shown no mercy. Mercy triumphs over judgment."

The phrase "Mercy triumphs over judgment" means that Christians who show mercy, those who are merciful towards others, will be vindicated at the judgment. To paraphrase: "It will go well" with them. They will be vindicated, exonerated, because they showed love for others and had mercy upon them. They did not show favoritism or partiality. So at the judgment, their love for others is taken into account and it goes well with them.

On the other hand, "judgment without mercy" is shown to "the one who has shown no mercy." If as Christians we have shown no mercy to others, then we can expect God to judge us the same way, "for judgment is without mercy to the one who has shown no mercy."

This seems to be the point of Jesus' teaching in Matthew's Gospel: "For if you forgive men their trespasses, your heavenly Father will also forgive you. But if you do not forgive men their trespasses, neither will your Father forgive your trespasses (Matthew 6:14-15)."

Similarly, Paul writes to Christians: "Be kind to one another, tenderhearted, forgiving one another, even as God in Christ forgave you (Ephesians 4:32)." Our tendency is to argue, "But they don't deserve it!" But that's the whole point of mercy. Like grace, mercy is being in a position of favor that is wholly undeserved.

In Matthew's Gospel, Jesus teaches about one particularly unmerciful servant. Let's allow Jesus to illustrate precisely what His half-brother James will teach later:

> The kingdom of heaven is like a certain king who wanted to settle accounts with his servants. And when he had begun to settle accounts, one was brought to him who owed him ten

thousand talents. But as he was not able to pay, his master commanded that he be sold, with his wife and children and all that he had, and that payment be made. The servant therefore fell down before him, saying, 'Master, have patience with me, and I will pay you all. 'Then the master of that servant was moved with compassion, released him, and forgave him the debt.

"But that servant went out and found one of his fellow servants who owed him a hundred denarii; and he laid hands on him and took him by the throat, saying, 'Pay me what you owe!' So his fellow servant fell down at his feet and begged him, saying, 'Have patience with me, and I will pay you all.' And he would not, but went and threw him into prison till he should pay the debt. So when his fellow servants saw what had been done, they were very grieved, and came and told their master all that had been done. Then his master, after he had called him, said to him, 'You wicked servant! I forgave you all that debt because you begged me. Should you not also have had compassion on your fellow servant, just as I had pity on you? 'And his master was angry, and delivered him to the torturers until he should pay all that was due to him.

"So My heavenly Father also will do to you if each of you, from his heart, does not forgive his brother his trespasses (Matthew 18:23-35)."

So our Heavenly Father will treat *us* if we fail to love our neighbor, fail to show mercy, fail to treat anyone "without partiality."

What About You?

In Matthew 5:43-47, Jesus says: "Bless those who curse you, do good to those who hate you, and pray for those who spitefully use you and persecute you...for if you love [only] those who love you, what reward do you have, or what good is that?" How is it possible to love those who don't love you?

Why is it not possible for a person to be saved by obeying the Ten Commandments?

What will happen to Christians on the day of judgment? What can you personally expect on that day?

❋ ❋ ❋

Chapter 10: Dead Faith, Living Faith
(James 2:14-19)

14 What does it profit, my brethren, if someone says he has faith but does not have works? Can faith save him?
15 If a brother or sister is naked and destitute of daily food,
16 and one of you says to them, "Depart in peace, be warmed and filled," but you do not give them the things which are needed for the body, what does it profit?
17 Thus also faith by itself, if it does not have works, is dead.
18 But someone will say, "You have faith, and I have works." Show me your faith without your works, and I will show you my faith by my works.
19 You believe that there is one God. You do well. Even the demons believe—and tremble!

Few weeks go by that we do not hear about some horrible tragedy that grips us and causes us to respond in shock and disbelief—a terrorist bombing, an airplane crash, a hurricane or tornado claiming the lives of hundreds of people. Immediately upon hearing the news, we offer up prayers for victims and families, shaking our heads in genuine compassion and sympathy.

And yet, tragic as these horrible events are, there is a far greater tragedy with which we live every day of our lives. There is a far greater tragedy in terms of eternal consequences that far exceeds the boundaries of mere physical concerns. This tragedy is to believe that one's soul is safe only to die with a false sense of spiritual security.

James warns us to examine whether our faith is genuine. He addresses the reality that there are many who live from day to day assuming that they are okay spiritually when they are not. He writes about faith here, genuine faith. And he contrasts *living* faith, real Christian faith, with what he terms a *dead* faith. We too should soberly consider his warning, allowing him to ask us: "Do you have genuine saving faith, or do you have a dead faith, a useless faith?"

One of the ways to better understand what something *is*, is by taking time to consider what that something *is not*. Let us consider these three truths about authentic, saving faith.

Saving Faith is not Merely Confessional

Saving faith, real Christian faith, is not merely confessional. That is, we are not Christians merely because we *profess* or *confess* to be. We are not Christians merely because we *say* that we are.

Here's how James puts it. He asks, "What does it profit, my brethren, if someone *says* (emphasis added) he has faith but does not have works? Can (this) faith save him?"

Right from the start James teaches that no one is a Christian based upon mere verbal confession. This teaching is reminiscent of the teaching of our Lord Jesus who said in the Sermon on the Mount, in Matthew 7:21 and following:

Not everyone who says to Me, "Lord, Lord," shall enter the

kingdom of heaven, but he who does the will of My Father in heaven. Many will say to Me in that day, "Lord, Lord, have we not prophesied in Your name, cast out demons in Your name, and done many wonders in Your name?" And then I will declare to them, "I never knew you; depart from Me, you who practice lawlessness! (Matthew 7:21-23)."

Merely *saying* we are Christians does not necessarily mean that we *are* Christians. Saving faith is not merely confessional.

James' immediate concern here is that there were some in the church who *said* they were followers of Christ, but the way they lived suggested otherwise. Principally, James teaches that these who said they were Christians did not "live it out," did not demonstrate that they were true Christians by showing concern for others.

He then provides an illustrative example: "If a brother or sister is naked and destitute of daily food, and one of you says to them, 'Depart in peace, be warmed and filled,' but you do not give them the things which are needed for the body, what does it profit?"

What *does* it profit? In other words, "What good is *that* kind of faith?" What good is there in a faith that is merely confessional? A man may *say* he is a Christian, but that proves nothing, especially if he clearly is not *living* as a Christian.

Suppose you see a man or woman dressed in shabby clothes and clearly hungry. You may feel very spiritual about yourself when you say, "God bless you! May you be warm and no longer hungry!" James protests: "But you do not give them what they need!" You don't give them food and clothing. James asks, "What good is that?!"

And he concludes that this kind of faith (the meaning of the question: "Can faith save him"), this *kind* of faith, this *useless* faith, is no good at all because it does not lead to action. This sort of faith does not lead to the good deeds one expects from Christians. In fact, James refers to this kind of faith as both "useless" and "dead." This is not the kind of faith that saves a soul. It is a faith "by itself," a faith that does not result in works.

So James concludes, "Faith by itself, if it does not have works, is dead." If it is a dead faith then it obviously cannot grant life. It does not lead to eternal life.

Saving faith is not merely confessional. We are not Christians simply because we *say* we are. We demonstrate that we are true Christians by the way we live.

This surely comes as no surprise to those who are genuinely saved. We understand that the power of the gospel leads to regeneration, new life. Jesus says we are "born again." We are, as Paul teaches, "New creations." He says, "If anyone is in Christ, he is a new creation; old things have passed away; behold, all things have become new (2 Corinthians 5:17)."

If we are truly saved, God gives us a new heart with new desires. We read the Bible because we desire to read the Bible. We attend worship because we desire to attend worship. We pray because God has given us a desire to joy in talking with Him. We give monies to the church not because we *have* to, but because we *want* to. We love God and we just naturally live out our Christian faith. Good deeds accompany our faith as evidence of new desires.

So James argues then that if a person says he has faith but does not have the accompanying good deeds that follow, then that person has every reason in the world to doubt whether or not he or she has been genuinely converted. Saving faith is not merely confessional. It is a confession that leads to expression, namely the doing of good deeds or works. "Faith by itself, if it does not have works, is dead."

We should pause for a moment to make clear that James is not contradicting the Bible's teaching elsewhere that a person is saved by grace alone through faith alone in Christ alone. Were we to disregard context and just pull a couple verses from different parts of the Bible, then it might appear as though there were a contradiction.

Were we to read James' statement: "Faith by itself, if it does not have works, is dead" and then open Paul's letter to the church at Ephesus and read: "For by grace you have been saved through faith, and that not of yourselves; it is the gift of God, not of works, lest anyone should boast (Ephesians 2:8-9)," we might conclude that James is teaching a "faith-plus-works" salvation and that Paul is teaching a "faith-minus-works" salvation. Is there a contradiction?

What we must understand is that James and Paul are speaking about two *different points* in the Christian life. Paul is talking about the way *into* the Christian life, the *beginning* of Christian living. James is talking about a point *after* one has become a Christian, the *living out* of Christian faith. We have made this point extensively: James does not write this letter to teach how to *become* a Christian, but how to *behave* as a Christian. Paul, in his writings, frequently stresses the way one *becomes* a Christian and he does so by teaching that the way to God's approval is not to be found in the way many of his Jewish acquaintances erroneously believed: by keeping the law.

Paul is addressing the entry point into salvation when he writes: "For by grace you have been saved through faith, and that not of yourselves; it is the gift of God, not of works, lest anyone should boast (Ephesians 2:8-9)." That is, "You cannot earn your way into heaven. You cannot 'work' your way into favor with God. You are saved by grace, through faith, in Christ, alone."

In that same passage, however, Paul goes on to say that once a person *is* saved, then he or she will live out the Christian faith by doing the good deeds and works that God has prepared. To the believer, Paul writes: "For we are His workmanship, created in Christ Jesus for good works, which God prepared beforehand that we should walk in them."

So salvation is not a "faith-plus-works," nor a "faith-minus-works," but a "faith *that* works." In the words of a popular proverb: "Faith alone saves," but "the faith that saves is never alone."[11]

James continues to teach that saving faith is not merely confessional. In verse 18 he suggests, "But someone will say, 'You have faith, and I have works.' Show me your faith without your works, and I will show you my faith by my works."

This verse is notoriously difficult to translate. In the original Greek manuscripts there is no punctuation and all the letters are side-by-side with hardly any space between them. Consequently, we cannot say for sure just *who* is doing the talking and *when*. We know that one person says something and that someone else responds. Beyond this, we cannot say for certain where the quotation marks rightly belong.

For our purposes it seems helpful to avoid being too near-sighted and back up a bit, reading the text in its wider context. This way—however the punctuation works out—the wider point remains: faith and works are inseparable. As wrong as it is for one person to say, "I have merely faith," it is equally wrong for the other person to say, "I have merely works." The two are inseparable.

Again, salvation is not a "faith-plus-works," nor a" faith-minus-works," but genuine living faith is a" faith *that* works." Faith alone saves, but the faith that saves is never alone; it will be accompanied by works that show this faith to be genuine, saving faith.

So if one person merely has good deeds; good works only and no faith, then this is a person who may be good on the outside, but has not been changed on the inside.

Have you ever heard the phrase, "empty suit?" An empty suit is a derogatory expression, a way of referring to someone who looks good on the outside—they're dressed nicely—but they are empty on the inside. Or we might say, "The lights are on, but there's nobody home." What we mean is that this person looks okay on the outside, but there's a problem on the inside. They are lacking something.

Applied to James' teaching on faith, one makes an "empty claim" when he or she boasts merely of either faith or works. Both are necessary for genuine conversion to have taken place. We are saved by grace through faith in Jesus Christ alone. But once we are "born again," new creatures with new desires, we will live out the truth of our confession by doing the good works God has ordained for us to do (Ephesians 2:10).

Saving Faith is not Merely Intellectual

Not only is saving faith not merely confessional, but it also is not merely intellectual. James addresses those who may have their doctrine right, but again fail to live out that faith in the doing of good deeds. Saving faith then, is not merely a cerebral or intellectual experience.

Specifically James says, "You believe that there is one God. You do well. Even the demons believe—and tremble!"

A person can believe orthodox statements about the Christian faith and still be lost. A person can accept truth claims about God and still be destined for hell.

The statement: "You believe that there is one God" is an orthodox Christian statement. There is but one God! So James says, "You do well." But then he warns: "Even the demons believe (this)—and tremble!"

Even demons believe true statements about God, but this does not mean that they are in a right relationship with God. Saving faith is not merely intellectual. We are not put into a position of favor with God simply by agreeing with true statements.

True Christian faith, living faith, grips both the head and the heart. Genuine faith is both cerebral and cardiological. If faith is merely intellectual then it is faith that resides only in our heads. If, however, we recognize the depth of our sin, and throw ourselves upon the mercy of our Lord and Savior Jesus Christ, and surrender to Him as Lord, then something has happened on the inside. Something has happened in our hearts. We are different. We are changed. We are saved. And this saving faith leads to the doing of good deeds or works.

The great Puritan preacher and thinker Jonathan Edwards makes this point in a sermon preached on this verse.[12] His sermon is entitled, "True Grace Distinguished From The Experience Of Devils." Isn't that a great Puritan sermon title?! Edwards makes the point that, just like demons, man can know the various attributes of God and yet remain lost. Here are a few excerpts from the sermon:

> The devils know God's almighty power. They saw a great manifestation of it when they saw God lay the foundation of the earth…and were much affected with it. They have seen innumerable other great demonstrations of his power, as in the universal deluge, the destruction of Sodom, the wonders in Egypt, at the Red Sea, and in the wilderness, causing the sun to stand still in Joshua's time, and many others…

> So the devils have a great knowledge of the wisdom of God. They have had unspeakably more opportunity and occasion to observe it in the work of creation, and also in the works of providence, than any mortal man has ever had…

> Devils and damned men know that God is eternal and un-

changeable. And therefore they despair of there ever being an end to their misery. Therefore it is manifest, that merely persons having an affecting sense of some, or even of all God's attributes, is no certain sign that they have the true grace of God in their hearts.[13]

This is precisely the warning James provides: one can believe true statements about God and still be lost. Mere understanding of biblical truths is no guarantee of salvation. It is no guarantee that the saving grace of God is operative in the heart.

Saving faith is not merely confessional and not merely intellectual. But there is more:

Saving Faith is not Merely Emotional

Note the emotion indicated by the demons. James describes them this way: "Even the demons believe—*and tremble!*"

They shudder, they bristle. They move, they shake. They feel. One could say that when they are in the presence of God, they are very emotional. A lost person can feel awe in the presence of God.

Emotions are part of our being. We all "feel" certain ways in certain situations. Emotions themselves are not problematic. The problem is when we base the authenticity of our faith upon mere emotional experience.

It is dangerous to believe we are genuinely saved simply because we have (or don't have) an emotional experience of some kind. No one is saved merely because he or she feels a certain way. The fact is there are many days when the true Christian does not necessarily feel very good or very spiritual. Emotions come and go.

A lost person can feel the warmth of a church building. A lost person can feel the care and concern of others. A lost person can feel good when listening to congregational music. He can feel excited, happy, and even good about his spiritual condition.

Saving faith then, is not merely *confessional*, not merely *intellectual*, and not merely *emotional*.

So what *is* a sign that the true grace of God is working in our hearts? We are saved when we place our faith in Jesus Christ alone as Savior. We believe that we are sinners who can do nothing to earn God's favor. We repent, turning from our sin and turning to Jesus Christ, looking to Christ alone for acceptance with God—Christ's redemptive work on our behalf. And this genuine faith and trust in Christ alone leads to a different way of living. We are new creations and we live out our Christian faith through practical deeds and loving works.

Salvation is not "faith-plus-works," nor is salvation found in "faith-minus-works," but genuine living faith is a "faith *that* works."

What About You?

Does your faith in Christ involve both "head" and "heart?" If not, or if you are unsure, read the brief appendix at the end of this book: "Becoming a Christian."

How can you use this passage to help someone come to faith in Christ?

"Faith alone saves," but "the faith that saves is never alone." Do you agree with this statement? Explain and apply your answer.

Chapter 11: Faith That Does Not Save From Hell
(James 2:20-26)

20 But do you want to know, O foolish man, that faith without works is dead?
21 Was not Abraham our father justified by works when he offered Isaac his son on the altar?
22 Do you see that faith was working together with his works, and by works faith was made perfect?
23 And the Scripture was fulfilled which says, "Abraham believed God, and it was accounted to him for righteousness." And he was called the friend of God.
24 You see then that a man is justified by works, and not by faith only.
25 Likewise, was not Rahab the harlot also justified by works when she received the messengers and sent them out another way?
26 For as the body without the spirit is dead, so faith without works is dead also.

I t's a sobering fact that there is a kind of faith that may seem genuine, but is a faith that is useless, powerless, and dead. It is a faith that does not save from hell.

When we speak of "saving faith," we are talking about a kind of faith that puts us in right standing with God. Saving faith is faith in Jesus Christ, the One who lived a perfect life for us and died a substitutionary death in our place, so that we could be forgiven of our sin.

Apart from God's grace through saving faith in Christ, every one of us deserves death, hell, and eternal separation from God. To be "saved" is to be rescued from that awful predicament, rescued and made right with God so that one may enjoy abundant and eternal life.

James teaches that true faith, saving faith, is shown to be genuine by the "living out" of one's faith. A true Christian will do good works—not in order to earn God's favor; this is impossible —but a true Christian will do good works as a demonstration of the fact that his or her heart has been truly converted. Good deeds, or good works, necessarily flow from authentic faith. This is why James can say, "Faith without works is a dead faith."

James gives two examples from the Old Testament to make the point that real faith is proved genuine by the doing of good deeds, works that naturally follow and flow from a truly converted heart. These two Old Testament examples are the examples of Abraham and Rahab, a patriarch and a prostitute.

Consider a Patriarch's Faith

Abraham is the patriarch of believing Jews and Christians alike. He is the primary "Father figure" of the faith. So James uses this patriarch to illustrate that one's faith is proved genuine by the doing of good works.

Specifically, James asks, "Was not Abraham our father justified by works when he offered Isaac his son on the altar?" And he adds, "Do you see that faith was working together with his works, and by works faith was made perfect?"

The background of James' illustration is found in Genesis 15 and Genesis 22. In short, Genesis 15 is where we read of Abraham's faith and Genesis 22 is where we read that Abraham's faith was proved genuine by the doing of good works.

Genesis 15 describes that memorable occasion where God promised Abraham that his descendants would be as numerous as the stars in the sky. And the Bible says, "And Abraham believed God and it was credited to him as righteousness (Genesis 15:6)."

This is the same text James cites now in verse 23 where he writes: "And the Scripture was fulfilled which says, 'Abraham believed God, and it was accounted to him for righteousness.' And he was called the friend of God."

The Apostle Paul also cites this text in Romans 4, teaching that one is declared righteous solely by faith. He writes: "Abraham believed God, and it was accounted to him for righteousness (Romans 4:3)." When a person genuinely believes, surrendering to God, he is credited "righteous." Abraham took God at His word. He was saved by grace through faith.

This is a good a place for us to review that men and women throughout biblical history are saved the same way. In our day we are saved by grace through faith in Christ, looking *back* in time to the event of the cross, looking back to the Christ who *has* come. In Abraham's day, believers also were saved by grace through faith, as they looked *forward* in time to the Christ who *would* come. Whether on one side of the cross or the other, all persons are saved by trusting God, looking to Him in faith.

Abraham believed God (Genesis 15) and his faith was proved genuine by what he did (Genesis 22). And what was it that Abraham did in Genesis 22? This is that marvelous accounting of Abraham's giving visible evidence of his faith in God by obeying God's command to offer up his son Isaac upon the altar.

To summarize, God says, "Abraham, take your son, your only son Isaac, whom you love, and...offer him as a burnt offering..." And the Bible says that Abraham obeyed God and proceeded to do precisely what God had asked. You can read the full account in Genesis 22, but for our purposes know that God stopped Abraham before he sacrificed his son because He was merely testing Abraham's faith, testing to see whether Abraham would obey. And Abraham passed the test. This is why James can say that Abraham was called "the friend of God."

God was looking for evidence that Abraham's faith was genuine. He tested Abraham and Abraham passed the test by demonstrating that his faith was not merely confessional, nor merely intellectual, nor merely emotional, but that his faith was real and genuine. That's why James can say that Abraham's faith "was working together with his works, and by works his faith was made perfect, or complete."

So James concludes, "You see then that a man is justified by works, and not by faith only." That is, one way we can be reasonably certain that a person is saved is by seeing the evidence of his or her genuine faith. If a person is born again, he or she will live a different life than before conversion.

It is important to note that no one can know for certain about the salvation of another. None of us can see into the heart the way God can see. But we can be reasonably certain that a person is saved if his confession of faith is demonstrated by the way he lives out his faith. There will be a growing pattern of godliness, an evidence of saving faith. The once barren tree now bears fruit. There is life.

How sad are those occasions when we attend a funeral and listen to a preacher trying his best to put a positive "spin" on the deceased person's life. We are told this man was a Christian. Perhaps even years earlier this person himself—like the person described by James in James 1:14ff—had "said" that he had faith. But there is no evidence, no overall pattern of spiritual growth. There is no real evidence of his love for God, nor love for His Word, the Bible. Here is a man who had faith, but apparently it was a faith James describes as useless, powerless, and dead. It was a faith that does not save from hell.

Abraham's faith saved from hell. His faith led to demonstrable works. We have learned from this patriarch's faith.

Consider a Prostitute's Faith

James could not have provided a greater contrast with Abraham than Rahab. He takes us from a patriarch to a prostitute, from a Jew to a Gentile, from a man to a woman, from one who was privileged to one who was poor, from one who had a good reputation to one who had a bad reputation.

He asks, "Likewise, was not Rahab the harlot also justified by works when she received the messengers and sent them out another way?"

The second chapter of Joshua relays the story of Rahab the prostitute. Rahab is the one who hid the spies, or messengers, that Joshua sent to do reconnaissance work in Jericho, the ones who viewed the land that they would soon be claiming as their own.

The Bible indicates that Rahab had come to know the One True God. She had heard how God had divided the Red Sea so that His people could cross over as they escaped the Egyptians. Rahab trusted in the One True God. So when God in His providence guided the spies to Rahab, she hid them so they would not be discovered by the unbelieving rulers of Jericho. Rahab risked her life by covering for the spies and helping them to escape later.

So Rahab, along with Abraham, serves as an example of one

whose faith in God was proved genuine by the doing of good deeds. Her works, namely her saving of the spies, proved her faith to be genuine.

I think it is a mark of grace on the part of James to place Rahab alongside Abraham. It is as if he wished to stress that whether one is "really good" or "really bad," both are saved the same way —by grace through faith, a faith that is proved genuine by the doing of good works. And a "really good" person like Abraham is no *more* saved than a "really bad" person like Rahab. And a "really bad" person like Rahab is no *less* saved than a "really good" person like Abraham.

Whether you identify more with Abraham the patriarch or Rahab the prostitute, every person is saved the same way and, because of the gospel, every Christian is on equal footing in the eyes of God. Every Christian—whether patriarch or prostitute —is loved equally by God because every believer is equally "in Christ."

If we are saved, God loves us perfectly in Christ. No one is *more* loved or *less* loved due to background, giftedness, education, or experience. Furthermore, no Christian will be loved *more* by God when he does well and no Christian will be loved *less* by God when he stumbles. God loves each Christian perfectly because He loves each one in His perfect Son Jesus Christ.

We've considered a patriarch's faith and a prostitute's faith. Thirdly and finally:

Consider a Powerless Faith

James concludes his argument by stating: "For as the body without the spirit is dead, so faith without works is dead also."

If you have ever viewed a dead body, you know exactly what James is talking about. You can tell the person's spirit is no longer there. There is nothing inside to animate the body. It is without spirit and dead. James says in a similar sense "faith without works is dead also." Faith without demonstrable works is like a dead body with no spirit. There is no life. There is no power.

But where there is genuine faith, saving faith, real living faith, there is power! It's interesting to note that when James speaks of the "works" of Abraham and Rahab, he does not have in mind the kinds of works which are generally familiar. James does not say, for example, "The reason Abraham and Rahab's faith is clearly genuine is because of their works of reading the Bible and going to church."

No, the "justification by works" evidenced in Abraham and Rahab are the "works" of putting their hopes and their very *lives* on the line for God. Abraham is willing to see his son die. Rahab risks her life by hiding the spies. These two people have anything but a powerless faith! They have a *powerful* faith, a faith that leads to life-denying, risk-taking works.

When you truly love someone, you will risk everything to be with that person. It's not that you are selfishly motivated by what you can get out of the relationship, but that you find pleasure and joy in simply being in the relationship.

I love this statement about Abraham at the end of verse 23: "And he was called the friend of God." When we are genuinely saved, we are regarded as a friend of God. We once were enemies of God, but by the grace of the gospel, we are now friends of God. What a wonderful relationship!

A person is not your friend if they are using you to get what they want, taking advantage of your position or the stuff you have, or your job. A true friend won't manipulate you to get what they want. Friendship is just being with someone because you love that person. It's the pure joy and pleasure of being in that relationship.

That's what being a Christian is like. We are friends *with* God and friends *of* God. We are His friends not for what we can get out of the relationship, but merely because we enjoy being with Him, being in His presence. Arguably, this desire to be with God is the greatest evidence of genuine salvation.

What About You?

If someone asks you how people in the Old Testament were saved, how would you respond?

How can you use the examples of Abraham and Rahab this week as you share the gospel with an acquaintance?

Our desire to be with God and spend time with Him is arguably "the greatest evidence of genuine salvation." Do you agree? Why or why not?

Chapter 12: So You Want to Teach the Bible?

(James 3:1-2)

1 My brethren, let not many of you become teachers, knowing that we shall receive a stricter judgment.
2 For we all stumble in many things. If anyone does not stumble in word, he is a perfect man, able also to bridle the whole body.

When you visit your family doctor one of the first things he asks you to do is to stick out your tongue. Then he carefully examines your tongue. Apparently our tongues reveal much about our physical bodies. I understand that a coated tongue may mean we have a fever and a yellowish tongue may indicate there is something wrong with our digestive system. Examine the tongue and you can make reasonable inferences about one's physical health.

In a similar way, our tongues reveal much about our spiritual health. The tongue is often a spiritual indicator of our hearts. The way we use our tongue, the way we speak, indicates something about who we are as a person and what we think of others. Someone said the tongue is the "tattletale of the heart."

We noted earlier that Jesus taught as much in Matthew's Gospel. He said, "Those things which proceed out of the mouth come from the heart…For out of the heart proceed [things like] evil thoughts…lies…blasphemies (Matthew 15:18-19)." The way we use our tongues is indicative of our true character.

The works about which James is concerned in the immediate context (*cf.* James 2:20-26) include the "work" of our speech. Good *works* include good *words*. True Christians take care to control their tongues. James goes into great detail about the misuse of our tongue in much of chapter 3, but he opens this section by first warning those who use their tongues to teach.

James warns Christians of the danger of being teachers, specifically teachers of the Bible. Bible teachers and preachers, by virtue of the fact that they will be speaking a great deal of words, are therefore in great danger of misusing their tongues.

Teachers are Judged More Strictly

James writes, "My brethren, let not many of you become teachers, knowing that we shall receive a stricter judgment." James warns that those aspiring to be teachers and preachers of the Bible will face a stricter judgment than those who do not teach and preach the Bible.

Before we go further, note that James assumes all Christians are aware that they will face *a* judgment. The very fact that he writes of a "stricter judgment" for Christian teachers implies that there will be a judgment for *all* Christians.

This is not a judgment to be confused with the judgment of unbelievers. The Bible speaks of a judgment of non-Christians at the end of the age. Revelation 20:11-15, for example, mentions the "great white throne judgment," where unbelievers will be called to appear and, because they are not followers of Christ—

and because their names are not recorded in the Book of Life—will hear the Lord say, "Depart from Me, I never knew you (see Matthew 7:21-23)."

There is a judgment for all those who are not in Christ. It is a judgment that results in eternal separation from God, an eternity spent in hell as just punishment for sin. This is why we must turn to Christ to be saved. Jesus is the only way to avoid hell. There is no other way to enter heaven. Jesus says emphatically: "I am the way the truth and the life, no one comes to the Father except by Me (John 14:6)." We must turn to Christ to avoid the judgment upon all unbelievers, all non-Christians.

The believer; the follower of Christ, does not fear the great white throne judgment. The true Christian will not hear Jesus say, "Depart from Me, I never knew you" because the true Christian knows the Lord and is known by the Lord. The true Christian has been saved from the consequences of sin by faith in Christ. The righteousness of Christ has been imputed to the believer, credited to the Christian, so that he or she stands before God "in Christ Jesus."

As Paul says in Romans 8:1, "There is therefore now no condemnation to those who are in Christ Jesus." Christians are "in Christ Jesus," justified; positionally secure and saved.

So the Christian will not face *condemnation*, but the Christian will be judged regarding his or her *sanctification*. We noted this truth earlier in Chapter 9. Entrance into heaven is not the concern for the believer on judgment day. His concern, rather, has to do with the degree of rewards—or loss of rewards. Every Christian will give an account of himself or herself before God (Romans 14:10, 12) and will receive rewards based upon the way he or she has lived (1 Corinthians 3:8).

To Christians, the Apostle Paul writes: "We must all appear before the judgment seat of Christ, that each one may receive the things done in the body, according to what he has done, whether good or bad (2 Corinthians 5:10)."

And just as there are degrees of punishment taught in the Bible, which includes degrees of punishment in hell, so there are degrees of reward taught in the Bible, which includes degrees of reward in heaven.

This prospect of reward or loss of reward in heaven causes many Christians to wonder what those rewards look like. What kind of reward will some have that others do not have? How can we truly be joyful if we find that we have lost some rewards?

Wayne Grudem is helpful here in his *Systematic Theology*. He writes:

> We must guard against misunderstanding here: Even though there will be degrees of reward in heaven, the joy of each person will be full and complete for eternity. If we ask how this can be when there are different degrees of reward, it simply shows that our perception of happiness is based on the assumption that happiness depends on what we possess or the status or power that we have. In actuality, however, our true happiness consists in delighting in God and rejoicing in the status and recognition that he has given us.

He adds:

> Those with greater reward and honor in heaven, those nearest the throne of God, delight not in their status but only in the privilege of falling down before God's throne to worship him (see Revelation 4:10–11)."[14]

As we turn back now to James' opening words in the text, we may ask why teachers will receive a "stricter judgment" than others. Surely it stands to reason that teachers of the Bible will receive a stricter judgment because they are handling the very Word of God. With great privilege comes great responsibility. Jesus says in Luke's Gospel, "Everyone to whom much is given, from him much will be required (Luke 12:48)."

The teacher opens the Bible, God's Word, and endeavors to teach what God says. This is a sobering task. To misrepresent God or to add to the Word something God has not said is a scary prospect.

On a personal note this is one reason I am committed to expository preaching, especially verse-by-verse preaching through books of the Bible. Aside from its many practical benefits, verse-by-verse expository teaching is the method least likely to stray from the plain meaning of Scripture.

The preacher opens the Bible and merely "exposes" what is in the open Bible before the people. He expounds upon the Scriptures and all the hearers may follow along and judge the accuracy of the exposition.

John Newton is known by many as the author of the hymn, "Amazing Grace." But Newton was also a pastor for a number of years. Indeed he was a Bible-teaching pastor who challenged his hearers to compare his teaching with what they read in their open Bibles:

> I count it my honor and happiness that I preach to a free people who have the Bible in their hands. To your Bibles I appeal. I entreat, I charge you to receive nothing upon my word any farther than I can prove it from the Word of God. And bring every preacher and every sermon that you hear to the same standard.[15]

Handling Scripture is a tremendous responsibility of Bible teachers and preachers. We must use the Word of God accurately and with integrity. It is the pastor's greatest responsibility. In the periodical, *Reformation & Revival,* Pastor Phil Newton agrees:

> The preacher must expound the Word of God or else he has failed in his calling. He may be a wonderful administrator, a winsome personal worker, and effective leader. But if he fails

to expound the Word of God, he is a failure to his calling to preach the Word.[16]

Indeed, preaching and teaching the Word of God is an enormous responsibility. This is to say nothing of the responsibility of those who *hear* the Word of God. If God places great stress on the *teaching* of the Word, what of the responsibility of those who *hear* and *listen* to its teachings?

James has already cautioned that Christians are to be "doers of the Word and not hearers only (James 1:22)." He takes for granted that Christians are actually in a position to "hear" the Word. This is a reasonable assumption. Christians are those who are interested in hearing from God by listening to the teaching of His Word. Once they have heard it, James argues, they must "do" it, living out its truths.

Teachers are Likely to Stumble

James is talking here about the likelihood of a Bible teacher's stumbling in speech, making a slip of the tongue. He says, "For we all stumble in many things. If anyone does not stumble in word, he is a perfect man, able also to bridle his whole body."

Stumbling is a metaphor for sinning. To stumble is to fall, or slip up. James' honesty is refreshing: "For we all stumble in many things." We all sin. Then he adds: "If anyone does not stumble in word (or speech) he is a perfect man, able also to bridle the whole body."

The word "perfect" is best understood in this context as "mature." The one who does not stumble as much as others in word, by what he says, is the one who has control over his tongue. He has control over his words. He or she is careful when speaking. This is a mature person who thinks before speaking and chooses words carefully, and considers how his or her words will be heard.

Teachers and preachers are in the business of using words to expound the Word. We teach God's Word by using our words so it just stands to reason that, the more words we use, the more likely we are to "stumble," to slip up, to say something erroneous or untrue. This is precisely what Solomon seems to suggest in Proverbs 10:19: "Where words are many, sin is not absent (NIV)."

If you are teaching the Bible, you may say things you didn't even realize you were saying. You can sin accidentally by saying something without thinking it through.

Mark Twain famously noted: "The difference between the *right* word and the *almost* right word is the difference between *lightning* and the *lightning bug.*"

What James issues as a warning to teachers is applicable to all Christians. We are all likely to stumble in speech. More about that in the next chapter.

What About You?

What if everything you said last week were recorded and played back next Sunday morning for your church family to hear? How does this hypothetical question motivate you to live this week?

How might a church use James 3:1-2 as a teaching tool for those eager to teach Bible studies in their church?

What method of preaching do you believe to be least likely to stray from the meaning of Scripture? Why?

❈ ❈ ❈

Chapter 13: Using Words Wisely
(James 3:3-12)

3 Indeed, we put bits in horses' mouths that they may obey us, and we turn their whole body.

4 Look also at ships: although they are so large and are driven by fierce winds, they are turned by a very small rudder wherever the pilot desires.

5 Even so the tongue is a little member and boasts great things. See how great a forest a little fire kindles!

6 And the tongue is a fire, a world of iniquity. The tongue is so set among our members that it defiles the whole body, and sets on fire the course of nature; and it is set on fire by hell.

7 For every kind of beast and bird, of reptile and creature of the sea, is tamed and has been tamed by mankind.

8 But no man can tame the tongue. It is an unruly evil, full of deadly poison.

9 With it we bless our God and Father, and with it we curse men, who have been made in the similitude of God.

10 Out of the same mouth proceed blessing and cursing. My brethren, these things ought not to be so.

11 Does a spring send forth fresh water and bitter from the same opening?
12 Can a fig tree, my brethren, bear olives, or a grapevine bear figs? Thus no spring yields both salt water and fresh.

We use our mouths every day. We speak at home, we speak at work, we speak at school, we speak to our neighbors, we speak to our children, we speak to our spouses. Some spouses are challenged by the words they use with one another. Some couples are challenged to speak at all!

A married couple awakened one Saturday morning and, like most mornings, had very little to say to each another. The phone rang and the wife answered. Her girlfriend Sally was on the other end so the two chatted awhile. After some time, she asked Sally what she and her husband were doing. Sally replied, "Oh, we're just sitting here having coffee and talking to each other." She hung up the phone and looked over at her husband who was reading the newspaper. She said, "Do you know what Sally and her husband were doing this morning? She said they were just having coffee and *talking* to each other! Isn't that great? I wish we would do that." Her husband peered over his newspaper and replied, "Well, we can do that. Put a pot of coffee on." His wife brewed some coffee, poured a cup for her husband and for herself. Then, after the two sat in silence for a full minute, the husband impatiently barked, "Well, call Sally up and find out what they were talking about!"

Truth is, for most of us it's not what we *don't* say that gets us into trouble, but what we *do* say. We are far more likely to use too many words than use too little. Solomon wisely advises: "The prudent hold their tongue (Proverbs 10:19; NIV)."

If Jesus is known for the "Sermon on the Mount," James is known for his "Sermon on the *Mouth!*" Nowhere else in all of the New Testament do we have such comprehensive treatment on the danger of the tongue.

In this passage, James describes four main characteristics of the tongue.

The Tongue is Influential

Influence can be used for good or bad. This seems to be what James is teaching as he develops his exposition on the tongue. He writes:

> Indeed, we put bits in horses' mouths that they may obey us, and we turn their whole body. Look also at ships: although they are so large and are driven by fierce winds, they are turned by a very small rudder wherever the pilot desires. Even so the tongue is a little member and boasts great things.

James likens the tongue to a bit used in a horse's mouth. This tiny piece of metal is placed in the mouth of a horse in order to guide it in the direction desired by the rider. Just a slight tug of the reins and that little bit causes the horse to stop, go, or turn one way or the other.

James then compares the tongue to the rudder of a ship. While ships are huge and driven by forceful winds, they are controlled "by a very small rudder wherever the pilot desires." The captain at the helm turns the wheel and the rudder responds so that the entire ship changes direction.

Such power! It's amazing when you think of the great influence of something so small.

James says just as the behavior of the horse is influenced by the little bit, and just as the behavior of the large ship is influenced by a small rudder, so the behavior of a person is influenced by the small tongue.

The tongue "boasts of great things." It is influential. It is capable of great things, things we should be using it for like praising our Lord, preaching the Word, or speaking well of others.

But the context of this passage tells us that while the tongue can be used in a positive manner, too often it is used negatively. While the tongue is capable of accomplishing "great things," too often we use it to bring about "great damage." To this problem James now turns.

The Tongue is Inflammatory

The tongue has the potential to arouse anger and hostility. It is incendiary and fiery. So while the tongue has the ability to "boast great things," James marvels, "See how great a forest a little fire kindles!"

Just as a small fire spreads and does great damage, so the tiny little tongue is capable of spreading damage far and wide. The tongue has the same potential as a little match has when lit and placed near dry, wooden brush.

Several years ago a 10-year-old boy admitted that he had started one of the largest wildfires in Southern California when he was playing with matches. The blaze, called, "The Buckweed Fire," started in the rural community of Agua Dulce:

> ...fanned by high winds and hot, dry weather...spread quickly, driving 15,000 people from their homes, destroying 21 houses and 22 other buildings, injuring three people and [burning] more than 38,000 acres."[17]

It all began with one match. James says your tongue has the same potential. Just one word. One small word spoken in anger has the potential to do the same destruction. "How great a forest a little fire kindles!" James adds:

> And the tongue is a fire, a world of iniquity. The tongue is so set among our members that it defiles the whole body, and sets on fire the course of nature; and it is set on fire by hell.

Interestingly, the word "hell" here is used only twelve times in the New Testament. Jesus uses it eleven times in His teachings in the Gospels and then James uses it here. Jesus referred to hell as the place of final condemnation. It is the place where non-Christians will spend eternity, the place where unbelievers are separated eternally from God because of their sin.

Here is a reminder of the need to have our sins forgiven, our need to turn away from sin and turn to the only Savior, the Lord Jesus Christ, the One who lived for our righteousness and died as a substitute to atone for our sins. The only way to avoid hell is to turn to Jesus Christ and to live for Him.

The tongue is inflammatory. Years earlier, Solomon warned of the same deadly potential of the tongue. He said:

> Without wood a fire goes out; without a gossip a quarrel dies down. As charcoal to embers and as wood to fire, so is a quarrelsome person for kindling strife (Proverbs 26:20-21; NIV).

Your tongue has the potential to ruin the reputation of others. When you repeat hearsay, when you repeat gossip, or when you fail to direct a critical person to go and talk directly with the person about whom he or she is criticizing, you are using your tongue in a way that tears down rather than builds up.

The tongue is influential and the tongue is inflammatory. But there is more:

The Tongue is Incorrigible

James says:

> For every kind of beast and bird, of reptile and creature of the sea, is tamed and has been tamed by mankind. But no man can tame the tongue. It is an unruly evil, full of deadly poison.

If you have visited the zoo or have been somewhere like Sea World, you likely have marveled at man's ability to tame all kinds of creatures. Both lion and lion tamer are in the same cage. Elephants gently place their foot upon a man's body. Dolphins jump through hoops to the delight of a watching crowd.

James suggests that it is remarkable that man can tame these wild animals, but is not so good at taming his own tongue.

Yet surely James does not mean that man is left without a solution. Surely he is not just ranting, concluding that nothing can be done about the matter. Indeed, it is by God's grace and our sanctifying growth in Christ that we are able to control our tongues. After all, "what is impossible with man is possible with God (Luke 18:27)."

Humanly speaking "no man can tame the tongue." Left to our own devices we are incapable of "breaking it" and taming it successfully and consistently. We are sinners! No amount of grit and human effort will finally culminate in our overcoming the unruly tongue. This is James' point.

He describes the incorrigible tongue as "an unruly evil, full of deadly poison." Like an arrow with a poisoned tip ready to be shot at one's enemies, so are the words we shoot at others, words "full of deadly poison."

We must watch our words, how we talk to others, how we talk to our children, our spouse, our neighbors, our co-workers, our fellow church members. To quote Solomon: "He who holds his tongue is wise (Proverbs 10:19; NIV)."

Some are proud of their ability to "tell it like it is." Like the woman who approached the great Methodist evangelist John Wesley and boasted, "Mr. Wesley, I pride myself in speaking my mind. That," she added, "is my talent." Wesley replied, "Well ma'am, the Lord wouldn't mind if you buried that talent!"

The tongue is influential, the tongue is inflammatory, and the tongue is incorrigible. Finally:

The Tongue is Inconsistent

James notes the irony that with the same tongue we praise God and then turn right around and say something that destroys others. We are inconsistent in using our tongue for good. He writes, "With it we bless our God and Father, and with it we curse men, who have been made in the similitude of God."

How inconsistent we are with our tongues! We gratefully exclaim, "Praise God" or "God is good" and then immediately spew hateful invective upon a person who has wronged us. One moment we are using our tongue for good and the next for evil. And when we speak evil of others, we are guilty of "cursing men who have been made in the similitude (or likeness) of God."

When you speak evil of another person, you are verbally attacking someone made in the image of God—believers and unbelievers alike. There is no other creature on the planet who is more like God than a human being. There is a very real sense, then, that when you and I speak hatefully about another person that we are speaking hatefully about God Himself.

Incredulously James states, "Out of the same mouth proceed blessing and cursing. My brethren, these things ought not to be so." We can almost picture James saying these words. Shaking his head, he lifts his hands palms upward as if to grasp for something he can't find, and then proclaims to any who will hear him, "These things ought not to be so!"

He is right, of course. These things ought not to be so. Yet how often are we guilty of doing the very things God forbids? We can be singing praises in a worship service and then, immediately after worship, approach another church member and engage in gossip. Moments earlier we were singing, "I'm so glad I'm a part of the family of God," and now we are using that same tongue to speak inappropriately about one of the family members. These things ought not to be so.

To further illustrate the utter inconsistency with which we use our tongues, James draws upon nature. Rhetorically he asks, "Does a spring send forth fresh water and bitter from the same opening?" And of course the implied answer is "No" as indicated by his conclusion: "Thus no spring yields both salt water and fresh."

A modern day equivalent might be something like, "When you turn on your kitchen faucet does it produce both fresh water and salt water?" Of course not! So just as a spring (or kitchen faucet) produces only one kind of water, so our tongues should be used to speak in only one kind of way. We should consistently use our words in a helpful way rather than a harmful way.

Mixing metaphors, James proves the point further by interposing questions related to horticulture. He asks, "Can a fig tree, my brethren, bear olives, or a grapevine bear figs?" Again, the implied answers are "No, of course not!" No one has ever seen a fig tree that bears olives instead of figs or a grapevine that produces figs instead of grapes.

James is using absurdity to illustrate the tragic inconsistency of the tongue. We should use our tongues consistently, using our words only for good and never for evil.

Danny Akin, president of Southeastern Baptist Theological Seminary, illustrates how inconsistent use of the tongue harms families:

> Such inconsistency compromises our confession, and in the family it can scar our children. Have you ever stopped to think what it is like to be a child and hear some of the things they hear coming out of the mouth of mom and dad? The same mouth that hopefully says, "I love you, I'm so proud of you, I thank God He gave you to me," may also be heard to say, "Shut up. Put that down. Stop that right now. I don't care what you are doing, come here right now. Listen to me. Give me that. Don't touch that. Not like that, stupid. Go away. Leave me alone. Can't you see I'm busy? Boy, that was really dumb. Can't you do anything right? You'd lose your head if it wasn't screwed on. Hurry up, we don't have all day! What's

the matter with you? Can't you hear anything? I don't know what I'm going to do with you. You will never grow up to amount to anything." And with words like these we don't bless, we curse. We don't build up, we tear down. And parents, words are powerful when directed at our children.[18]

Let us conclude James' teaching on the tongue by endeavoring to do three things in the coming week. May this be our daily prayer as we ask for God's help.

1) Think before I Speak

Someone has encouraged our asking the following questions[19] before we open our mouths to speak. Before we say what we're going to say, we are wise to first ask ourselves:

Is it True?
Is it Kind?
Is it Necessary?
Does it improve upon the silence?

2) Use My Words to Edify

To edify is "to build up." We should always speak in ways that "build up" another person, helping them, rather than "tearing down" that person with our words.

3) Encourage Others to Do the Same (No Gossip)

We help others when we refuse to engage in negative criticism or gossip. We also help others by lovingly correcting them when they speak this way. When a person begins to speak to you this week in a way that is harsh or critical of another person, remind them that Jesus teaches to go to that person directly with their criticism (Matthew 18:15-17). Tell them, "Do as Jesus says. Go to that person directly and share with them." And be sure that you yourself do the same.

What About You?

Do you see an overall pattern of improvement in the use of your tongue? If not, what does this mean and what will you do about it?

How does the secular world operate regarding James' teaching on the tongue? In other words, do you think successful CEOs speak the way James urges?

What are ways you can use your tongue this week to edify a spouse or a child or another family member?

Chapter 14: Your Wisdom: Heavenly or Un-heavenly?
(James 3:13-18)

13 Who is wise and understanding among you? Let him show by good conduct that his works are done in the meekness of wisdom.
14 But if you have bitter envy and self-seeking in your hearts, do not boast and lie against the truth.
15 This wisdom does not descend from above, but is earthly, sensual, demonic.
16 For where envy and self-seeking exist, confusion and every evil thing are there.
17 But the wisdom that is from above is first pure, then peaceable, gentle, willing to yield, full of mercy and good fruits, without partiality and without hypocrisy.
18 Now the fruit of righteousness is sown in peace by those who make peace.

I ronically, our first parents, Adam and Eve, stumbled at the point of wisdom. Tempted by Satan to eat of the Tree of the Knowledge of Good and Evil, they disobeyed God by reaching for the forbidden fruit in hopes of becoming wise:

> So when the woman saw that the tree was good for food, that it was pleasant to the eyes, and a tree desirable to make one wise, she took of its fruit and ate. She also gave to her husband with her, and he ate (Genesis 3:6).

This one act of disobedience brought sin to the entire world (Romans 5:12-21).

Reviewing the actions of Adam and Eve is helpful to us in our study of James' text. We have by nature an inclination to chase after a wrong kind of wisdom, a godless wisdom, a counterfeit wisdom, a wisdom that "does not descend from above" but rather from below, a wisdom that is "earthly, sensual, (and) demonic."

You might say that this is the kind of wisdom we have "by default." It is part and parcel of our sin nature. Therefore, apart from regeneration and conversion, we will give expression to this wrong kind of wisdom through our words and deeds. What is within us by nature manifests itself outwardly.

Recalling the context of James' teaching on the tongue aids our reflection upon the source of wisdom. You will recall from the last chapter James' pointing out the inconsistency of the way in which we use our tongues. With our tongue "we bless our God and Father, and with it we curse men, who have been made in God's likeness (verse 9)." And James illustrates this inconsistency by encouraging us to consider a natural spring from which flows two kinds of water, both good and bad.

The reason two kinds of water flowing from one source is absurd is precisely because spring water can flow from only one source. Applied to the use of our tongues, the source of our words flows from the "source" of our hearts. Our words are a reflection of what is inside us.

Jesus taught this in Luke's Gospel. He said, "Out of the abundance of the heart the mouth speaks (Luke 6:45)." The tongue reveals what is in the heart. Or, to paraphrase a bit from Mark's Gospel, "It's not what goes in your mouth and into your stomach that defiles you; you are defiled by what comes from your heart and out of your mouth (Mark 7:15)." The words we speak are an indication of what's in our hearts.

So James turns now to this matter of wisdom. He writes about two kinds of wisdom, each of which flows from one kind of heart or the other. He describes both a biblical wisdom and an unbiblical wisdom, a heavenly and an earthly wisdom. The heavenly wisdom flows from a heart that has been changed by God. The other kind of wisdom is a wisdom that flows from a godless heart, an unchanged heart, a heart James actually describes as demonic. James doesn't pull any punches!

Let's endeavor to consider the kind of wisdom James says we should have: "wisdom that is from above," a biblical wisdom, or heavenly wisdom. Let's consider three characteristics of this heavenly wisdom.

It is Displayed by Good Conduct

Biblical wisdom is displayed, or shown, by the Christian's conduct. Put another way: heavenly wisdom is not so much what one *knows*, but how one *lives*.

This makes sense given James' emphasis on the practical expression of our Christian faith. We recall that this letter is a letter of action, a letter about living out the faith. James says, "Don't be merely a hearer of the word, but a doer of it." James is like someone from Missouri, the "Show Me" state! He wants us to show our faith, display it, and live it out. Heavenly wisdom is displayed by good conduct.

James asks, "Who is wise and understanding among you?" Perhaps some listening to the public reading of James' letter would raise their hands in response. If so, we would expect James to say, "Put your hands down. You can prove you are wise and understanding by the way you live." To quote James precisely: "Let him show by good conduct that his works are done in the meekness of wisdom."

The word "good" translates a Greek word that describes something beautiful. It is the same word found in our English word "calligraphy," beautiful writing. In a sense, then, James is saying, "Do you want to know how you can tell whether someone has biblical wisdom? They are the ones who live beautiful lives before others."

You don't have to have physical beauty to live a beautiful life before others. Similarly, there are a lot of people who have physical beauty, but the way they live is ugly.

Remember that James is not teaching that an unbeliever is put in right standing with God by his conduct. He is not teaching that one is saved by his works, earning God's favor and approval through good works. James is addressing those who have already embraced the gospel. He is writing to those who know that they cannot earn God's favor because—in Christ—they already have it. And that is what motivates them to live out the Christian life, a beautiful life.

This godly wisdom is distinguished from what is best described as a counterfeit wisdom, a wisdom that is not "from above," but is rather a godless wisdom from *below*.

It is Distinguished from a Godless Counterfeit

James describes this godless, counterfeit wisdom. He says, "But if you have bitter envy and self-seeking in your hearts, do not boast and lie against the truth." He adds, "This wisdom does not descend from above, but is earthly, sensual, demonic."

This earthly wisdom is the wisdom Satan wants us to embrace. He desires that we exchange heavenly wisdom with un-heavenly wisdom, a worldly wisdom that focuses on self. James adds that if all we possess is worldly wisdom then we should not "boast and lie against the truth." In other words, if we possess earthly wisdom we have absolutely nothing about which to brag.

One of the ways James describes this earthly wisdom is with the phrase "self-seeking in your hearts." Self-seeking connotes the idea of "selfish ambition," an ambition with little to no regard for others. It is a willingness to be divisive, or to divide a group, to marginalize or alienate others in the interests of one's own desire for power or prestige.

This is much the way the world operates. We see it in business, in politics and, unfortunately, even in religion. Too often there is a willingness to split the group in order to achieve what one person wants. And the sense is, "I really don't care how this affects you all, I'm going to do this because it is what I want."

James concludes his description of this "wisdom that does not descend from above" by stating: "For where envy and self-seeking exist, confusion and every evil thing are there."

Such is the chaotic disorder of earthly wisdom. It is in diametrical opposition to godly wisdom. It is a godless counterfeit. Rather than focusing upward toward God, it focuses inward toward self.

What have we learned thus far about biblical wisdom? It is displayed by good conduct and it is distinguished from a godless counterfeit. Finally:

It is Defined by Godly Characteristics

James concludes his exposition by giving no fewer than eight characteristics of heavenly wisdom. He states, "But the wisdom that is from above is first pure, then peaceable, gentle, willing to yield..."

What James has written thus far seems to go totally against

modern notions of success and advancement. "Willing to yield?" Who does that?! Isn't that a sign of weakness?! Americans, for example, are a proud nation of rugged individuals. We may bristle at calls for compromise and gentle behavior. At the same time, however, if we identify with Jesus Christ, then we must always remember that we are first Christians before we are anything else.

If we follow Christ we will live out our faith in ways that often, if not usually, go against the grain. He who is wise is always "willing to yield" out of deference and respect for others.

Derek Prime, pastor for many years in Edinburgh, Scotland, made a statement once about the Christian's willingness to yield. As he and a younger minister were on their way to an important meeting at the church, a meeting were there was going to be a number of varying opinions, Prime remarked: "It's one thing to know your mind, it's another thing to have your mind made up."[20]

If we have our "minds made up" before we ever enter into a meeting, whether it's a meeting of a group, or a one-on-one meeting, and we enter into that meeting with a smug, self-assured, "I know I'm right" sort of spirit, then, even if we *are* right, we're in no position ever to learn anything. To have a spirit that is "willing to yield" means we humble ourselves, are teachable, and willing to learn.

When I was ten years old our family moved from California to Georgia. It was at the end of my 5th grade year and I was getting acclimated to my new school. I had learned to play trumpet in California and felt I was pretty good. So as I made my way to my first band practice in Georgia I was really disappointed. The band was not assembled by ability, but by grade. I remember thinking, "Man, this is pretty pathetic. I need to be in the 6th or 7th grade band." To make matters worse, while I was "first chair" in California, my new band director automatically assigned me to the fourth part. The part was well beneath my ability and I remember being frustrated, feeling like I had fallen to a new low.

After practice I approached my new band director and said, "I'm sorry, Mr. Brown, but in California we were playing stuff a lot harder than this and I'm used to playing first part." I remember well his sobering reply. He said, "A really good trumpet player will play any part assigned him."

Sometimes God forces us to learn how to yield! Biblical wisdom means we have humility, we're teachable.

James continues to describe this wisdom from above as "full of mercy and good fruits, without partiality, and without hypocrisy." He adds, "Now the fruit of righteousness is sown in peace by those who make peace."

Those who make peace—peacemakers—are those who reap a harvest of righteousness. So again, biblical wisdom is not about self, it's about others.

One of the keys to being a peacemaker is found in the preceding verse where James says that biblical wisdom is "full of mercy and good fruits." If you are full of mercy then you can extend mercy to others. You have a limitless supply of mercy.

When another Christian hurts you, you've got plenty of mercy to give out. A helpful parallel is a verse to which we have previously referred, Ephesians 4:32: "Be kind to one another, tenderhearted, forgiving one another just as God has forgiven you in Christ." Because God has shown you mercy, so you can show mercy to others.

Christ's atonement for our sins puts us in a position to forgive the offenses of others. Because of the gospel, Christians can affirm confidently: "God has forgiven all of my sins, all sins past, present, and future. I am no longer guilty of sin."

If this is true, and it is, think about how your forgiveness from God applies to your forgiving others. We are quick to think about how God's grace and mercy applies to us individually, but think also about how God's grace and mercy applies to other Christians with whom you may find yourself at odds.

In other words, consider how God's forgiveness of another Christian's sins may include His forgiveness of that person's sin against *you*. So if *God* forgives that person's sin against you, should you not *also* forgive that person's sin against you?

This is a major key to overcoming bitterness. Whatever hurt that Christian may have inflicted upon you—or may yet inflict upon you—consider it a sin for which God has forgiven him at Calvary. God forgives him just as He forgives you. You then, also forgive him based upon Christ's atoning sacrifice.

What About You?

How does popular wisdom of the world differ from God's wisdom?

Are you "willing to yield" or teachable?

How can God's forgiveness of your sin move you to forgive those who have hurt you?

Chapter 15: The Ease of Becoming God's Enemy
(James 4:1-6)

1 Where do wars and fights come from among you? Do they not come from your desires for pleasure that war in your members?
2 You lust and do not have. You murder and covet and cannot obtain. You fight and war. Yet you do not have because you do not ask.
3 You ask and do not receive, because you ask amiss, that you may spend it on your pleasures.
4 Adulterers and adulteresses! Do you not know that friendship with the world is enmity with God? Whoever therefore wants to be a friend of the world makes himself an enemy of God.
5 Or do you think that the Scripture says in vain, "The Spirit who dwells in us yearns jealously"?
6 But He gives more grace. Therefore He says: "God resists the proud, but gives grace to the humble."

M any of us are familiar with the so-called "boiling frog metaphor." It is a graphic metaphor used to illustrate how change can occur over time. The idea is that if you wish to cook a frog you cannot simply throw a live frog abruptly into a pot of boiling water. If you were to try to do so the frog would feel the drastic heat of the water and immediately jump out of the pot. On the other hand, if you place the frog in a pot of warm or tepid water, he'll stay in the pot while you slowly and gradually turn up the heat. Over time, you are able to cook the frog successfully because the frog has acclimated to his environment, totally oblivious to the fact that he is being slowly cooked to death.

Whether this actually happens to frogs is a matter of debate. I have never tried it and don't intend to! Contemporary biologists have challenged the accuracy of the anecdote but most agree that the metaphor itself is helpful, if not powerful. Change to a person's environment is easier to accept when it is introduced gradually, incrementally, or subtly, over time.

It reminds me of the way a friend described the moral failure of a Christian. We often speak of a person's "fall into sin" and my friend said, "No one really *falls* into sin. He *slides* into it." It is gradual, it is subtle. It happens incrementally, over time. One compromise leads to another compromise and then to another still. Before long, like a frog in a pot of increasingly warmer water, we find ourselves immersed in a situation that may well end in death.

This is a helpful metaphor as we study the above text. James warns of the ease of becoming God's enemy. He declares: "Friendship with the world is enmity with God." Friendship with the world puts one in opposition to God. James adds, "Whoever therefore wants to be a friend of the world makes himself an enemy of God."

We often use the term "worldliness" to describe the kind of person James has in mind, a person who is more inclined to follow the ways of this fallen world rather than the ways of the Lord. Worldliness is a lifestyle James describes in the previous chapter as earthly, sensual, and demonic.

There is a real warning here in this text that applies to every one of us. Few of us would willingly jump into sin like a frog thrown into a pot of hot water. No one wants to ruin his life. I doubt any true Christian wakes up each day and thinks, "Gee, I think I'll get arrested today. I think I'll commit adultery today and bring shame upon the Lord and His church, ruin my Christian testimony, and lose my family." Such thinking is ludicrous.

On the other hand, we may give in to one "small" temptation that leads to another. Then a second temptation leads to a third, then another, and so on. And gradually, subtly giving in to smaller incremental changes over time, we allow ourselves to embrace the world and, before long, have "cooked ourselves." This is the ease of embracing worldliness and becoming God's enemy.

Some of us may be in a pot of water right now and we don't even know it. We don't realize it. So, in an effort to help us recognize worldliness, and help us "jump out of the pot" if you like, let's study the above verses, looking for warning signs of worldliness, indicators that we may be far more comfortable with a world opposed to the things of Christ than we realize.

There are at least three main characteristics of wordiness in this passage. Let us consider each one carefully.

Unhealthy Cravings (Self-Centeredness)

Deep within each and every one of us are desires. And these desires can be either good or bad; healthy or unhealthy. James is concerned about unhealthy cravings. He asks, "Where do wars and fights come from among you? Do they not come from your desires for pleasure that war in your members?"

We recall from the previous chapter that James concluded his discourse on heavenly wisdom by describing it as, among other things, "peaceable (James 3:17-18)." Now James describes the opposite of peace with reference to "wars and fights" among the Christian community.

The word "members" is best understood as "parts of your body" or more generally, "that which is within you."

The New Living Translation is helpful here: "What is causing the quarrels and fights among you? Don't they come from the evil desires at war within you?" Here is the source of worldly divisiveness among Christians: evil desires, unhealthy cravings within.

Specifically, James describes these unhealthy cravings as "desires for pleasure." The word "pleasure" here is the word from which we get hedonism, a self-centered focus or an unhealthy craving for that which merely satisfies self. James teaches that these passions lurking within us have the potential to work outside us such that we find ourselves at odds with other people. We "make war" with other people in the church. So the *cravings within* lead to *conflict without.*

We have noted previously that the way we act on the outside is driven by the way we think on the inside. Unhealthy cravings within lead to conflict without. Self-centeredness leads to divisiveness. Self-centeredness leads to "making war" with one another in the church.

The King James Version translates verse 1 this way: "From whence come wars and fightings among you? Come they not hence, even of your lusts that war in your members?"

When we read the word "lusts" we often think only of sexual lust. To be sure, sexual lust is one of the unhealthy cravings within that leads to conflict without. If you have an unhealthy desire to satisfy yourself, that unhealthy desire tempts you to look at others in an unhealthy way. In the sexual realm, an extreme obsession with selfish and self-centered gratification can lead to an extreme case of physical "warring and fighting" such as rape or other abuse. It begins with unhealthy cravings. Cravings within lead to conflict without.

But James has more in mind than mere sexual lusts. There are other lusts, other cravings within; lusts for power, or position, or wealth, or evil desire for status and recognition.

A bitter and resentful inward focus, for example, can turn one into a hater of mankind. Bitter people are often given to narcissism, an unhealthy focus on the pride of self and an expectation that others should regard them as superior. When others do not, we may expect "wars and fights" of shunning, finger-pointing, whispering, and so on.

All of this, says James, is driven by "desires for pleasure that war in your members," desires for the pleasure of self satisfaction, self amusement, self importance, self gratification, and more. Unhealthy cravings within lead to conflict without.

The second warning sign of worldliness is ungodly conduct which is marked by divisiveness.

Ungodly Conduct (Divisiveness)

Self-centeredness leads to divisiveness. James puts it this way: "You lust and do not have. You murder and covet and cannot obtain. You fight and war."

We have noted earlier that the original New Testament contains no punctuation. That's a helpful reminder here because these short statements in verse 2 can be a bit confusing no matter which English translation we are using. I think verse 2 may be better translated this way:

"You lust and do not have, so you murder. You covet and cannot obtain, so you fight and war."[21]

James is showing us how unhealthy cravings within lead to ungodly conduct without. You lust and do not have (within), so you murder (without). You covet and cannot obtain (craving on the inside), so you fight and war (conduct on the outside). Unhealthy cravings within lead to ungodly conduct without.

William Barclay explains helpfully:

> The craving for pleasure drives men to shameful deeds. It drives them to envy and to enmity; and even to murder. Before a man can arrive at a deed there must be a certain driving emotion in his heart. He may restrain himself from the things that the desire for pleasure incites him to do; but so long as that desire is in his heart he is not safe. It may at any time explode into ruinous action.[22]

The *New York Times* published an article about the recent discovery of a bomb in Germany that led to the evacuation of 20,000 people in Berlin. The people were evacuated so that the bomb could be disarmed. The bomb was discovered along the Rhine River during excavations for a pipeline. It was a bomb that had been dropped seven decades earlier by the Allies during World War II. The article explains that there are many of these bombs lurking beneath the surface of places all over Germany. In the previous year, in one of the most populace places of Germany, bomb squads defused nearly one thousand bombs alone.[23]

In a similar way, every person has lurking within themselves the potential of an explosion without. The Christian has been liberated from the *power* of sin, but not the *presence* of sin. While sin no longer *reigns*, it *remains*. To grow in holiness, Christians must correctly deal with sin every day of their lives. If we don't regularly confess our sin and turn from our sin, we may "go off" like a bomb that was previously lying dormant and has suddenly found ignition.

The key to keeping these bombs from going off is to defuse them regularly by finding satisfaction in healthy ways rather than unhealthy ways, by finding ultimate satisfaction in Christ and His perfect will for our lives.

A person who is divisive is a person who is not well on the inside. This is a person who has unresolved issues of self-centeredness or an overblown sense of self-importance. This is a person who craves self-recognition and acts out divisively when those unhealthy desires are not met. Unhealthy cravings within lead to ungodly conduct without.

Next, James says, "Yet you do not have because you do not ask."

Here is a reminder that Christians should ask God for the things they seek rather than allowing their unhealthy cravings to lead them into sin. Of course, James is not teaching that God grants our selfish desires. That is clear based upon what he says in the very next verse: "You ask and do not receive, because you ask amiss, that you may spend it on your pleasures."

Don't ask God for things to satisfy your unhealthy cravings. Don't treat God as something of a divine "To-Go Window," approaching Him hurriedly and "placing your order" thinking only of what you want. Someone said this is like "using God as a means to your own end rather than seeking God as the end itself."

Instead of seeking God to satisfy our unhealthy cravings, approach Him in humility, asking for things consistent with His will. Ask for things that bring glory to Him. Ask for things that He believes are best for you and others. We must ask in accordance to God's perfect will for our lives. This is the kind of prayer that God honors and delights to answer!

We should note also that James is not teaching that *all* pleasures are wrong. Only pleasures inconsistent with His will are wrong; pleasures that do not glorify Him.

Remember that the very last verse of the opening chapter of the Bible says: "Then God saw everything that He had made, and indeed it was very good (Genesis 1:31)." Everything God created "was very good."

Not all pleasures are wrong. Sexual intimacy, for example, is a pleasure given by God to be enjoyed within the sole context of biblical marriage, the union of one man to one woman. The pleasure of sex is wrong only when used in a context other than biblical marriage.

Again, we are to come to God asking for things that are consistent with His will. When we come to God in this way the very act of prayer itself has a sort of purifying effect upon us. It calls into question the health of our desires. It prompts us to consider: "are these things for which I am asking healthy cravings or unhealthy cravings?"

James now provides the third warning sign of worldliness:

Unholy Compromise (Unfaithfulness)

James teaches that worldliness is, in essence, spiritual adultery. Like a trial attorney concluding his case, James thunders:

> Adulterers and adulteresses! Do you not know that friendship with the world is enmity with God? Whoever therefore wants to be a friend of the world makes himself an enemy of God.

Equating worldliness with adultery is a concept rooted in the Old Testament. God is regarded as the Husband of Israel and Israel as God's bride. To be unfaithful to God is to commit spiritual adultery.

This is the same truth Jesus taught in Matthew's Gospel: "No one can serve two masters; for either he will hate the one and love the other, or else he will be loyal to the one and despise the other...(Matthew 6:24)" You can't be faithful to both God and the world. Put another way: you can't have two spouses.

If you are married, imagine your spouse taking a few hours of each day to go over to another person's home, a person of the opposite sex, and spending a few hours alone in intimacy with that person. He or she comes back to you each day and says, "Oh, we're just friends." You protest, "Yes, but you are *with* that person and you expect me to just be okay with it?!" Nearly every one of us understands just how wrong that would be. This sort of "friendship" with others is nothing less than infidelity and unfaithfulness.

This is precisely the point James makes with his rightful accusation: "Adulterers and adulteresses!" God regards our friendship with the world as infidelity to Him. When we are worldly, we are adulterers and adulteresses. You might say we are "prostituting" ourselves. We are sleeping around. We are unfaithful to the One True God.

This truth is developed in the next verse: "Or do you think that the Scripture says in vain, "The spirit[24] who dwells in us yearns jealously"?

The idea here is that God places within us an inner spirit that is properly satisfied only when we are reconciled to God and only when we find complete satisfaction in God Himself. The NLT has: "God is passionate that the spirit he has placed within us should be faithful to Him."

James appears to be summarizing the teachings of the Bible on this matter when he refers to "the Scripture." It's as though he were asking, "Do you believe the teaching of the Bible to be wrong here—the idea that God has created us for relationship with Him and that we should be faithful?"

When we compromise our convictions and we allow ourselves to be pulled away from God by the tug of the world, then we are committing spiritual adultery. We are allowing the spirit within us to find satisfaction in other "spouses," things other than God Himself.

Verse 6 points us to the cure for worldliness, a cure, or correction to be developed more fully in the verses to follow. James says, "But He gives more grace. Therefore He says: 'God resists the proud, but gives grace to the humble.'"

God is always ready to give grace to those who come to Him in humility. When we come before God with a desire to be faithful to Him and to grow and to find satisfaction in Him, He gives us the ability to live in a way that both pleases Him and blesses us.

When we ask God to disentangle us from the ways of the world, He gives us the grace to be disentangled. We have to ask ourselves, however, whether we really want to be disentangled from the ways of the world.

Do you really desire Him more than anyone or anything? Or do you want it both ways: a little of God and a little of the world? Do you really want a vibrant and committed relationship with God or do you want to "sleep around a bit?" You're glad to drink from the living water, but you'd also like to drink occasionally from the broken cisterns of muddy water. Know the ease of becoming God's enemy and beware.

Don't settle for cheap substitutes of the One True and living God.

What About You?

Can you think of ways that the "boiling frog metaphor" applies historically to the people of God?

Do you have unhealthy desires of which you need to repent right now? If so, confess, repent, and ask God to give you desires for Him.

"A person who is divisive is a person who is not well on the inside." Do you agree with that statement? Are there ever occasions where divisiveness is necessary? Explain.

❋ ❋ ❋

Chapter 16: The Cure for Worldliness
(James 4:7-10)

7 Therefore submit to God. Resist the devil and he will flee from you.
8 Draw near to God and He will draw near to you. Cleanse your hands, you sinners; and purify your hearts, you double-minded.
9 Lament and mourn and weep! Let your laughter be turned to mourning and your joy to gloom.
10 Humble yourselves in the sight of the Lord, and He will lift you up.

In the previous chapter we examined the *cause* of worldliness. We turn now to the *cure* for worldliness. Before we do, it may be helpful to review what we have learned. To be "worldly" is to allow ourselves to love the things of this fallen world more than we love the things of the Lord. Worldliness according to James is friendship with the non-Christian world such that it makes one an "enemy of God (James 4:4)."

In the four verses above (verses 7-10), there are no fewer than ten commands, all imperatives in the original text. We have noted previously that James is fond of using the imperative mood likely because it fits his style. His letter is an alarming call to action and we are wise to heed its teachings.

We may summarize the cure for worldly living by observing three necessary actions. First:

Allegiance to the Right Person (Faithfulness)

Allegiance to the right person means allegiance to God. It means we are faithful to Him, separating ourselves from the encroachments of the world. James says, "Therefore submit to God. Resist the devil and he will flee from you."

To "submit" means "to arrange under," as in, "to arrange ourselves under the authority of another," and the idea is that of enlistment. We enlist in God's service. We do not enlist in the service of the enemy, namely the devil. Nor do we enlist in a half-committed way, giving some allegiance to God and some to the devil. We are to choose sides and remain faithful.

If we love the Lord then we will want to be faithful to Him. Love moves us to "arrange ourselves under" His authority.

The Apostle John teaches a similar idea in his first letter. He writes:

> Do not love the world or the things in the world. If anyone loves the world, the love of the Father is not in him. For all that is in the world—the lust of the flesh, the lust of the eyes, and the pride of life—is not of the Father but is of the world. And the world is passing away, and the lust of it; but he who does the will of God abides forever (1 John 2:15-17).

Paul also states in a familiar verse: "Do not be conformed to this world...(Romans 12:2)." JB Phillips paraphrases the verse memorably: "Don't let the world around you squeeze you into its own mold..." How easy it is to become increasingly comfortable with the ways of the world, allowing the world to change us rather than our changing the world.

What are some signs that we may be allowing the world to

squeeze us into its own mold?

We may show that we love the world more than we love the Lord by the way we think, speak, and live. Our idle thoughts may lead us into sinful thinking, lustful thoughts, thoughts of anger, resentment, and bitterness. Remember: what is inside the heart comes out. We've noted this truth in the last few chapters. If we have issues on the inside they'll show up on the outside. Wrong thinking leads to wrong living.

You may love the world more than the Lord if you find yourself too busy for Bible reading. You may love the world more than you love the Lord if you don't tithe or give generously.

You may love the world more than you love the Lord if you are too tired for corporate worship when the church gathers together. Frequently, Christians miss corporate worship because of love for the world, because they have allowed the things of the world to choke out their first love.

You may love the world more than you love the Lord if it's easier to gossip than it is to witness. You find it easier to talk to others about others than to talk to others about Jesus. You love the world more than you love the Lord if it's easier to look at pornography than it is to look at the Bible.

Allegiance to the right person means to be faithful to the Lord and "resisting the devil."

Interestingly, James' call to "resist the devil" is sandwiched between two positive commands: "Submit to God" and "Draw near to God." And right between those two commands is the negative command: "Resist the devil."

The key to resisting Satan is not merely to rebuke him, though rebuking the devil is a wise practice. When Jesus sensed the work of the tempter in his life, He said, "Get thee behind me, Satan (Matthew 16:23)."

But consider why the instruction of resisting the devil is sandwiched between the two great commands of submitting to God and drawing near to God. It's as though James is showing us the best way to resist the devil and ensure that he flees from us is by remaining especially close to God, submitting to Him and drawing near to Him. I love that promise in the first part of verse 8: "Draw near to God and He will draw near to you."

Do you want to feel the power of God's presence in your life? How much time did you spend last week drawing near to Him? Be honest. How much time did you spend last week just "hanging out" with friends, watching movies, or surfing the internet? How much time did you spend last week drawing near to God through prayer and the reading of His Word? How faithful have you been in worship?

If you want the feel the power of God's presence every day in your life, the answer is right here in this verse: "Draw near to God and He will draw near to you." And take care not to reverse the order. The promise of God's drawing near to you does not come before your drawing near to Him.

The first cure for worldliness is allegiance to the right Person (faithfulness). We turn now to the second cure:

Applying the Right Practice (Holiness)

You may recall from our last study that verse 6 says, "God gives more grace." God is faithful to give us whatever grace is necessary to practice holiness, growing in our faith and becoming more like Jesus. Grace is not only the source of the Christian's *salvation* but also the source of the Christian's *sanctification*. Grace not only *saves* us from a life in hell, grace *sanctifies* us for a life of holiness.

To be sure holiness does not always come easily. There is no holiness without effort. Growing in Christ requires discipline. So James commands: "Cleanse your hands, you sinners; and purify your hearts, you double-minded."

These terms "cleanse" and "purify" recall the Old Testament priests' washing their hands before entering the tabernacle (Exodus 30:17-21). Used by James, the terms convey the idea of having purity before God and others. It is a call for practical holiness and sanctified living.

To be "double-minded" is to have one's loyalty divided between God and the world. You can't have it both ways. As Jesus says: "You can't serve two masters (Matthew 6:24)." You can't love both the things of God and the things of the world.

Then James says, "Lament and mourn and weep! Let your laughter be turned to mourning and your joy to gloom."

I doubt this verse is anyone's favorite Bible verse! Imagine someone asking, "What's your favorite life verse?" And some guy replies dolorously, "Lament and mourn and weep! Let your laughter be turned to mourning and your joy to gloom."

Why is James saying this? Surely he is addressing those times in our lives when we are so in love with the world that we find ourselves laughing when we ought to be mourning.

Imagine attending a funeral where some man sitting on the front pew is laughing the entire time. You say, "That's inappropriate behavior! He should be mourning, not laughing." In essence, James is saying, "Yes, that's exactly what I'm talking about. There are times when your inappropriate behavior calls for mourning rather than laughing."

It's easy to laugh at a sitcom on TV or a movie full of immoral innuendo. Someone tells an indecent joke at work and you laugh. James says, "Lament and mourn and weep! Let your laughter be turned to mourning and your joy to gloom."

There are times in our lives where laughter is inappropriate. It is not that God never wants us to laugh or have joy. There is joy throughout the Bible! No one has more joy in life than a faithful Christian. But we cannot truly know the joy of the Lord if we are unfaithful.

Until we learn to mourn for our sin we will remain unchanged. If we persist in compromise and continue in worldliness, we will never grow in holiness and thus never know the true joy of the Lord.

The cure for worldly living is allegiance to the right person (faithfulness), applying the right practice (holiness), and thirdly:

Assuming the Right Posture (Lowliness)

James says, "Humble yourselves in the sight of the Lord, and He will lift you up."

This verse may be interpreted as a general principle, an echo of our Lord's teachings in the Gospels: "And whoever exalts himself will be humbled, and he who humbles himself will be exalted (Matthew 23:12)."

Given the context, however, it seems James would have us understand his call for humility as a necessary corollary of the command to "Lament and mourn and weep." Repentance is no laughing matter. If we are turning our joy to gloom then we will assume the right posture. We will assume a posture of lowliness.

I think the JB Phillips paraphrase best captures the flow of James' thought:

> As you come close to God you should be deeply sorry, you should be grieved, you should even be in tears. Your laughter will have to become mourning, your high spirits will have to become heartfelt dejection. You will have to feel very small in the sight of God before he will set you on your feet once more.

Here is a picture of humility! This final cure for worldliness is a call to assume the right posture, a posture of lowliness before the Lord. We are honest with Him. We admit that we have allowed ourselves to become entangled with the things of the world and we have been awakened to the danger of continuing down this path. We confess, repent, and draw closer to God.

What About You?

Can you identify some ways in which you are tempted to "allow the world to squeeze you into its own mold?"

What can you do the next time you find yourself laughing when you ought to be mourning?

Though certainly not Jesus' main point, how does the parable of the prodigal son (Luke 15, especially verses 17-20) illustrate James' teaching about drawing near to God, knowing He will draw near to us?

❋ ❋ ❋

Chapter 17: The Danger of Criticism
(James 4:11-12)

11 Do not speak evil of one another, brethren. He who speaks evil of a brother and judges his brother, speaks evil of the law and judges the law. But if you judge the law, you are not a doer of the law but a judge. 12 There is one Lawgiver, who is able to save and to destroy. Who are you to judge another?

A recurring theme in James' letter is the truth that what is in a Christian's heart is what comes out. In the words of Solomon: "As a man thinks in his heart, so is he (Proverbs 23:7)." Wrong thinking within leads to wrong living without. Evil *thinking* within leads to evil *speaking* without.

In this tiny paragraph of two verses James addresses the matter of speaking evil against a fellow Christian. To speak evil may also be rendered to "slander" as the NIV has it.

James instructs us as to the danger of slander, the danger of speaking in evil ways that "tear down" rather than "build up" (recall James 3:1-12). Two actions surface from a study of these two verses, two actions that will improve our communication with others.

Allow the Bible to Determine Your Communication

If you are a Christian, you will allow the Bible to provide the framework for the way you speak, the way you talk. James is clear, "Do not speak evil of one another..."

The verb translated by the words "speak evil" conveys the idea of speaking in a demeaning way of people when they are not present to defend themselves.

It is the idea of "talking down" another Christian, not "talking down to" another, but "talking down." It is the sense of tearing down, demeaning, belittling, even destroying another person. And again, it is especially the idea of doing so when that person is not present to defend himself or herself.

So it is the idea of talking to others about others in a way that does not help, but rather hurts. It is talking about another Christian secretively, spreading slanderous gossip to others about a person who is not present to address the speaker.

It may well be that the substance of the things said about another is true. Slander is not necessarily false. In fact, in this context, James could have used a different word to convey lying, but he does not. He is addressing bad communication that is, in essence, the speaking about another brother or sister in an unhelpfully critical way especially when that person is not present.

Have you ever done this? Have you ever spoken about another person who wasn't present to defend himself? Perhaps you spoke in a critical way that was demeaning of that person. In doing so you placed yourself in a morally superior position over the person about whom you were speaking.

Many of us are familiar with the legend of the dandelion. According to the legend, if you pick a dandelion and blow upon it and all of its seeds disappear, then your wish will come true. Of course it is just a legend, but the image is helpful. If you've ever blown upon a dandelion, you've watched it release a spray of those tiny little seeds which are carried away in a number of different directions. Trying to locate and retrieve those tiny little seeds would be next to impossible.

Speaking evil of another Christian is like blowing upon a dandelion. Your words spread in a number of directions as various people hear what you have said and then pass it along to someone else. Trying to "take back" your words would prove as difficult as trying to locate tiny dandelion seeds in a field.

Perhaps you would say you have never spoken evil of another Christian. Have you ever *listened* to someone speak evil of another? If so, you are culpable in an act that is ungodly and unbecoming of a Christian.

If someone turns to us and begins engaging in slander of another brother or sister, we must help by telling him not to speak to us if he is going to speak evil of another brother or sister. We must take this person to passages such as this in James 4:11 and lovingly explain that his behavior is wrong. We may also turn to passages such as Matthew 18:15 where Jesus says, "If your brother sins against you, go and tell him his fault between you and him alone." Never give a hearing to those who speak critically of other Christians, especially when those others are not present to defend themselves.

And be forewarned: someone has wisely said, "Whoever gossips *to* you, will gossip *about* you."

Is it always bad to talk about a person who is not present? Of course not! There are many occasions during a day when we will be talking about others. Allow me to share a helpful exercise to ensure that you always speak in edifying (to "build up") ways of others when they are not present. It's really simple: just imagine that the person is present when you are speaking about him. Picture him right there with you as you are talking to the other person. You are likely to be more fair, kind, and careful with your words.

One of the reasons it is wrong to slander a believer is because that believer is an actual brother or sister, a member of our Christian family, the family of God. The word translated "brethren" in verse 11 may be better translated "brothers and sisters," all members of the family of God.

Just as it is wrong for you to speak evil of a brother or sister in your *physical* family, so it is wrong to speak evil of a brother or sister in your *spiritual* family—in fact, it is arguably *more* wrong as your spiritual family is a family of those united in Christ, children of God, our Father.

As God's children, then, we are co-equal brothers and sisters. None of us is even firstborn! Only Christ is the firstborn (Romans 8:29) so no one has the right to "talk down" another brother or sister. We are all of equal stature. When we properly humble ourselves "we have no 'altitude' left from which to 'talk down' to anyone!"[25]

Your Christian brother or sister is your family. You take care not to speak evil of your physical family—your husband, your wife, your parents, your children—so you don't speak evil of your church family. You wouldn't be unfaithful to your physical family, so you won't be unfaithful to your church family. You don't get angry and walk out on your physical family, so you shouldn't get angry and leave your church family.

James argues that when Christians speak evil of other Christians they have become judgmental critics: "He who speaks evil of a brother and judges his brother, speaks evil of the law and judges the law. But if you judge the law, you are not a doer of the law but a judge."

He is addressing our fallen tendency to have a judgmental

spirit, placing ourselves in a morally superior position over our brothers or sisters.

Here is an important qualification: when James warns about "judging" a brother or sister, he is not saying that Christians are *never* to make moral evaluations. He is not saying that Christians are never to judge between right and wrong. James himself, in writing this letter, is making *many* moral evaluations! He is clear about what is right and wrong.

Similarly, when Jesus says, "Judge not that ye be not judged (Matthew 7:1-5)," He is not forbidding *all* judgment. In the very same passage where Jesus says, "Judge not that ye be not judged," He warns about false teachers (Matthew 7:15-20). Indeed, Jesus adds that the way one may determine whether teachers are false is by making a judgment about the kind of fruit they are producing; is it good or bad? This analysis requires moral evaluation, a judgment.

We must always beware of taking Bible verses out of context. To do so increases the risk that we will lose the meaning of the text. God's Word is powerful when rightly interpreted. Our desire always should be to determine the true meaning of a verse, and that meaning is often discovered simply by giving careful attention to the context.

Using verses out of context is in vogue in our culture. How many times, for example, have we heard someone appeal to Matthew 7:1 and cry: "You're not supposed to judge!" Is this really what the Bible teaches? Are we never once supposed to make a moral evaluation about whether something is true? Or whether someone's conduct is appropriate? Of course not.

The Bible certainly does not teach that Christians are to look the other way when a brother or sister sins. The Bible calls for addressing that sin carefully and lovingly (see Galatians 6:1-2).

James does not forbid making moral evaluations altogether. He is concerned about our having a judgmental attitude or a judgmental spirit. He is not forbidding a "judgment of truth," he is forbidding "being judgmental." It's an attitude of moral superiority, thinking of ourselves more highly than we ought.

Speaking in an unhelpfully critical way about another person makes oneself judge and jury. In speaking evil of others, not only are we placing ourselves in a position of moral superiority over another Christian, but we are also placing ourselves in a position of moral superiority over the Bible.

James says, "He who speaks evil of a brother...*speaks evil of the law and judges the law*."

It is as though we believe we know better than the Scriptures. We act as though we know better than the law, law such as Leviticus 19:16: "Do not go about spreading slander among your people (NIV)." Yet our sinful reasoning is:

> Well, I can slander if I please. I know better than the law. I know better than "the royal law" which is to love your neighbor as yourself (James 2:8). I don't really need to do that. It doesn't apply to me.

Wrong thinking within leads to wrong conduct without.

As Christians we must allow the Bible to determine our communication. Secondly:

Allow the Bible to Determine Your Limitations

Forgive the allusion to Clint Eastwood's character in the Dirty Harry movies, but a memorable quote from "Magnum Force" is where Eastwood's character Harry Callahan says, "A man's got to know his limitations."

While I couldn't recommend the movie for family viewing, I can say that that particular line is essentially what James is saying in verse 12: We've got to know our limitations.

We are incapable of placing ourselves in a high position of moral superiority over others because we're not that smart, we're not that good, and we're not that fair—in a word, we're not God!

When we have a judgmental spirit, we are acting as God. We are acting as though we are the ones to lay down the law. James corrects this thinking: "There is one Lawgiver, who is able to save and to destroy. Who are you to judge another?"

James is incredulous: "Who are *you*?!" Who do you think you are, placing yourselves in a high position of moral superiority over others? Do you think you're sinless? Do you think you've never done anything wrong? Or said anything wrong? Or made an unpopular decision? Do you really think you're *that* good? Who are you to judge another?!

"There is one Lawgiver." That one Lawgiver and judge is God. He is the only one "able to save and to destroy." Only God can both save and destroy in an ultimate sense; eternally save, eternally destroy.

God is the only one in a position of moral superiority. That's why God is the one who gives the law. Only God has the right to give biblical laws because God alone is consistently good, right, fair, and knows all things.

Would any one of us dare to claim that we are always good, always right, and always fair? Is there one of us who would dare claim that we know all things? Of course not. This is why there is no place for our acting morally superior to others. It's as though James were saying, "Frankly, you're not that good a person! You're not that smart. Know your limitations. You don't know everything about that person you are criticizing. You don't have all the facts."

See, when you judge another person by being critical and demeaning, you are acting like you have all the information about that person's situation. You're acting like you know and have all the facts.

James is warning against our jumping to conclusions and judging before all the facts are in.

A church member once gave me ways I could pray for her while she was away on a mission trip. She had written down a number of statements she wished to keep. Her plan was to review these statements each day and she had asked me to pray that she would keep them. One of the statements read: "I purpose to never assume I understand or know the motives of others."

That's a good statement. James is warning here against doing that very thing. By saying there is but one Lawgiver and by asking, "Who are you to judge another?" James is reminding us that we don't have all the information about another person's situation. We don't know that person's motives. We don't know why they acted the way they did or why they said what they said. We simply don't know. We're not that smart. We're not omniscient. In a word, we're not God.

Solomon warns in Proverbs 18:17: "The first to present his case seems right, till another comes forward and questions him." That's another way of saying there are times when we think we have all the information only to discover later that there was much we did not know.

We don't know everything. What is more, we ourselves are so often guilty of the very actions we condemn in others. Such knowledge should engender a greater humility within us.

The great Scottish preacher Alexander Whyte was a bold, yet humble minister known for his authentic, self-effacing manner. G.F. Barbour tells of one memorable occasion during Whyte's ministry:

> When he was speaking in a slum where its inhabitants were known for their drinking, he astonished his hearers by informing them that he had found out the name of the wicked-

est man in Edinburgh, and he had come to tell them; and bending forward he whispered: "His name is Alexander Whyte."[26]

What About You?

"You're not supposed to judge!" Is this true? Explain.

How do you feel about helping another Christian by not listening to gossip and encouraging their following Scripture? Are you comfortable doing this? If not, why not?

How does our "not having all the information about another person's situation" help us mind our tongues?

Chapter 18: The Uncertainty of Tomorrow
(James 4:13-17)

13 Come now, you who say, "Today or tomorrow we will go to such and such a city, spend a year there, buy and sell, and make a profit";
14 whereas you do not know what will happen tomorrow. For what is your life? It is even a vapor that appears for a little time and then vanishes away.
15 Instead you ought to say, "If the Lord wills, we shall live and do this or that."
16 But now you boast in your arrogance. All such boasting is evil.
17 Therefore, to him who knows to do good and does not do it, to him it is sin.

In the JB Phillips paraphrase of this passage, there is a heading right above the text that reads: "It is still true that man proposes, but God disposes." The idea is that man may plan the events of his life, but the God who is sovereign will do as He believes best. God's sovereignty precludes man's presumption. So "Man proposes, but God disposes."

This phrase is centuries old, apparently occurring first in Thomas à Kempis' 15th century classic, *The Imitation of Christ.* And you will find it in number of other places. In fact, if you do a Google Image search on the phrase "Man proposes, but God disposes" you will be directed to a 19th century oil-on-canvas painting by the English Painter Edwin Landseer.

In the painting by the same title, Landseer depicts the aftermath of a ship lost in the arctic sea and the ensuing disappearance of 129 men, explorers who had sailed in 1864 in search for the Northwest Passage. The ship and the men disappeared into the arctic ice. Man proposes, God disposes.

God's sovereignty precludes our presumption. This really is at the heart of what James is teaching in these verses. Most pressing on his mind is the presumptuous planning of Christian merchants, but his warning applies universally to all people in all times and in all situations: God's sovereignty precludes man's presumption. Solomon put it this way in Proverbs 16:9, "In his heart a man plans his course, but the Lord determines his steps."

Let us turn now to James' text and examine it more closely, noting no fewer than three facts about life.

Life Consists of Uncertainty

This point is unmistakably present in the words of James. He cautions: "Come now, you who say, 'Today or tomorrow we will go to such and such a city, spend a year there, buy and sell, and make a profit…"

James has in mind primarily Christian merchants or businessmen; men who travel and trade goods and services for profit. We may picture a man unfurling a huge map, flattening it out on a table and pointing to various places of interest where he hopes to go in order to "buy and sell, and make a profit."

On the surface there is nothing wrong with this kind of thinking and planning. We all plan events and give thought to the days ahead in terms of what we hope to do or accomplish. There's nothing wrong with having a day timer or using the calendars on your computers or smartphones. In fact, because God is an orderly God, there is something of our mirroring our Creator when we plan our days and structure our lives. Created in God's image, our orderliness reflects the glory and grandeur of an orderly God.

Planning the future is not the problem. But what then *is* the problem? Fundamentally, it is the problem of presumption. It is the brazen and arrogant way we may plan our days and events as though we were in charge of everything and that everything we plan will come to pass.

A key to understanding what is wrong in verse 13 is to consider not so much what is *said* but what is *not* said. Indeed, the key to understanding what is wrong with the presumptive boast of the one speaking in verse 13 is to consider what he leaves out—or better still, *who* he leaves out.

When you read verse 13, do you see any reference at all to the One True and Living God? No. There is no mention of Him. And lest we become too critical, how much of our own lives do *we* live or plan without giving so much as a thought to God's plans?

The futility of presumptuous planning is especially proven by the next verse: "whereas you do not know what will happen tomorrow…"

James sounds a bit like Solomon: "Do not boast about tomorrow, for you do not know what a day may bring forth (Proverbs 27:1)."

Who knows what tomorrow holds? Life is full of uncertainties. This truth can actually liberate us from so much fretting about and losing our temper when things don't go "our" way. Belief in the sovereignty of God—that God is absolutely in control and is overseeing all events for His glory and our good—means we can rest knowing that He is doing what is best. The Christian knows that God always does what is right, every single time without exception.

Frankly, the fact that we do *not* know what tomorrow holds is nothing short of a profound mercy of God. I'm not sure I *want* to know the future!

Thankfully, God knows what we can handle and what we can't handle. He knows for our own good whether to give or to withhold a happy providence. He also knows exactly when to unveil a trying or difficult circumstance meant to grow us and conform us to greater Christlikeness (Romans 8:29). God knows best and always acts rightly.

Life consists of uncertainty. Second fact of life:

Life is Characterized by Frailty

This is such a humbling truth! We are not as strong as we may think. James asks and then answers a question worthy of sober reflection: "…For what is your life? It is even a vapor that appears for a time and then vanishes away."

The Greek word translated "vapor" is an old word meaning "mist." It's the word from which we get our English word "atmosphere." Our lives are like that evanescent misty steam rising from our morning coffee. We see it but for a moment and then it is gone.

How foolish that we should speak so presumptuously about our plans for the future when our lives are so fragile, so fleeting, so frail.

Of course this does not mean we are to live our lives dejectedly, consigning ourselves to the fatalism of a meaningless existence. That is not what James is teaching! Quite the contrary: created in God's image we have real meaning and purpose. God has designed us to live our lives for His glory and when we live for Him we experience life on the most joyous level possible.

James gives us what we *ought* to say instead of boasting of our self-made, self-determined plans. Rather than saying, "Today or tomorrow we will go to such and such a city, spend a year there, buy and sell, and make a profit," James argues: "Instead you ought to say, "If the Lord wills, we shall live and do this or that."

"If the Lord wills." That's how we are to speak: "If the Lord wills, I will be alive tomorrow." Pretty humbling, right? Someone invites you to go somewhere, imagine you were to reply: "If the Lord allows me to live." Sounds kind of morose, doesn't it?!

I'm not sure that James actually means we are to say these exact words every time, but I do think he wants us to *think* this way every time. We are to be thinking this way, deep down in our hearts, knowing that our lives are full of uncertainties. We will only do this or that if the Lord permits.

The Apostle Paul thought this way. We see evidence of it in his first letter to the Corinthians. He writes, "I will come to you shortly, if the Lord wills (1 Corinthians 4:19)," and, "I hope to stay awhile with you, if the Lord permits (1 Corinthians 16:7)."

This is a healthy and humbling way to think: "If the Lord permits" or, "Lord willing." Christians of earlier generations would often conclude in their letters something of their plans and then append the Latin phrase, *Deo Volente*, God permitting.

Our lives are characterized by so much uncertainty and frailty. No one knows for certain what's going to happen tomorrow or in the next few hours. This truth takes us to the final fact of life:

Life Calls for Humility

It is the obvious response. The cure for presumptuous thinking, planning, and living is humility before God. James bemoans the lack of humility in his hearers: "But now you boast in your arrogance. All such boasting is evil."

Rather than saying, "If the Lord wills, we shall live and do this or that," the arrogant, prideful, if even "successful" businessman boasts, "I'm going to go and do this or that and make a profit," leaving God's sovereignty entirely out of the equation.

James says in verse 16, "You boast in your arrogance" and, "All such boasting is evil." The man who "boasts in his arrogance" is like the popular mountebank portrayed in old Western movies. You know the character: he's the fellow who has a cart full of various elixirs, nostrums, and potions. He jumps up on a soapbox and begins to boast about how he can cure this and fix that. And he can do nothing of the sort. He's a charlatan.

But we are no different when we "boast in our arrogance," planning the business trip without bathing it in prayer, seeking companionship without seeking God first, or preparing for a career without ever considering how God may be glorified in it. "All such boasting," warns James, "is evil."

So James concludes: "Therefore, to him who knows to do good and does not do it, to him it is sin." He is addressing what is frequently called a sin of omission. Most of us are aware of sins of *commission*, deliberate sins, the active doing of something we know to be wrong.

Sins of *omission*, on the other hand, are those occasions where we remain passive, leaving undone the things we ought to do. To quote James again: "to him who knows to do good and does not do it, to him it is sin."

Given the immediate context James is saying, "If you fail to humble yourselves and you continue to speak and act presumptuously, leaving God out of your thinking and planning, you have sinned."

Life consists of uncertainty and is characterized by frailty. Therefore, life calls for humility.

Let us conclude our study by asking a practical question: "Given what James teaches in these verses, how can I practice humility this week?" Consider three ways:

1) You are weak and fragile, so trust God with your life

Remember that you depend upon Him for everything. Everything! Food, clothing, shelter, rest. Our lives are a vapor, a mist, here for a moment and gone. We must depend upon God for everything.

2) You don't know everything, so trust God with your plans

Remember James warns: "You do not know what will happen tomorrow." Be humble: You don't know everything. You don't know the future.

Remember that not knowing the future is as much a *mercy* of God as a *mystery* of God. God knows what we can handle and when we can handle it. He knows whether to give or withhold information. He is always working, growing us and conforming us to greater Christlikeness. God knows best and always acts rightly.

So don't worry about the future and trust God with your plans.

3) You can't keep breathing forever, so trust God with your soul

This is a clear and blunt conclusion given James' teaching in these verses. Because our lives are like the evaporating steam rising from our morning coffee, we ought to say, "If the Lord wills, we shall live…"

Ultimately, God alone keeps us living. Ultimately, God alone keeps us breathing. How foolish we are if we do not trust Him with our soul and live for His glory.

I saw an image once in an online article that gripped me. The story was about efforts to revive someone whose heart had stopped beating. What struck me was the image: a couple of doctors or nurses standing over a man who was lying motionless on a gurney. One of the doctors was holding defibrillator paddles above the patient as though he had just tried to shock the patient's heart into beating again.

What was so gripping about the image was the look on the faces of the doctors as they stood over the patient. They stood motionless, their eyes fastened to the heart monitor, waiting to see whether the man's heart would start beating. Their frozen posture indicated that they had done all that was humanly possible to revive the man. There was nothing more they could do except watch to see whether the man's heart would beat again.

That image is a memorable reminder that ultimately God alone keeps us living and breathing.

Many of us grew up praying a certain bedtime prayer. The words have changed a bit over time. We now teach our children to pray it this way:

Now I lay me down to sleep,
I pray the Lord my soul to keep,
Guide me safely through the night,
and wake me with the morning light.

It's not a bad prayer. I used it myself when raising my boys. But as I've grown older I have gained a greater appreciation for the prayer I was taught when I was small:

Now I lay me down to sleep,
I pray the Lord my soul to keep,
And If I die before I wake,
I pray the Lord my soul to take*.*

I think that prayer is more honest, more humble in its petition. I believe it conveys a far better understanding of, and appreciation for, the God who is sovereign over the affairs of men—including His sovereignty over our very souls.

You are not going to go on breathing forever, so trust your soul to God.

What About You?

What part does God play in your plans for the upcoming week?

How can you use this passage when sharing the gospel?

How many sins of omission did you commit last week? Last hour? What does this teach about the human condition and our need for a Savior?

❋ ❋ ❋

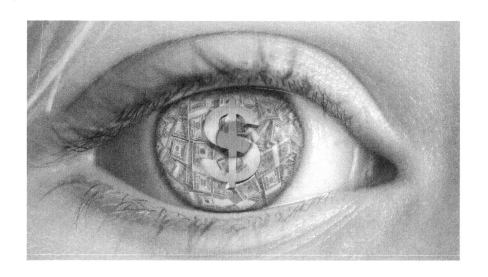

Chapter 19: When Money is our God
(James 5:1-6)

1 Come now, you rich, weep and howl for your miseries that are coming upon you!
2 Your riches are corrupted, and your garments are moth-eaten.
3 Your gold and silver are corroded, and their corrosion will be a witness against you and will eat your flesh like fire. You have heaped up treasure in the last days.
4 Indeed the wages of the laborers who mowed your fields, which you kept back by fraud, cry out; and the cries of the reapers have reached the ears of the Lord of Sabaoth.
5 You have lived on the earth in pleasure and luxury; you have fattened your hearts as in a day of slaughter.
6 You have condemned, you have murdered the just; he does not resist you.

Entering now into the last chapter of James' letter, we are met with a blunt warning to those who are rich. While James has in mind particularly wealthy landowners (who may not even be Christians), his warning applies universally to all people of all time.

To be wealthy is not a sin in and of itself. We never read in the Bible that a person is sinning merely by being rich. Job is a classic example, a man who was very wealthy. And God took away Job's wealth, but not because he was sinning. Indeed, the first verse of Job's story describes him as "blameless and upright, and one who feared God and shunned evil (Job 1:1)." There are other lessons in the Book of Job and it is not my purpose to teach them here, but the book ends with God's not only restoring Job's wealth, but giving Him twice what he had before. My point is simply that there is no sin merely in being rich.

James' most pressing interest is to warn against the danger of allowing money to take on a divine status. He warns against living for riches and oppressing others in the hopes of financial gain. He warns that God sees and knows all things and will judge us for our failure to use money wisely.

Let's examine these verses more closely, noting two discernible warnings that rise from the text.

Money may Deceive us

To be deceived is to be duped into believing something that is not true. The implicit deception addressed by James has to do with the judgment to come. James is saying that those who are rich—and again he has in mind wealthy landowners who were mistreating their laborers—are living in such a way as though there were no judgment to come. They are living as though Jesus were never coming back.

The deception is evident in the way James addresses these wealthy landowners: "Come now, you rich, weep and howl for your miseries that are coming upon you!" James' cry suggests that these rich folks were laughing when they should have been weeping, reminiscent of his earlier teaching: "Lament and mourn and weep! Let your laughter be turned to mourning and your joy to gloom (James 4:9)."

It's as though James were saying, "You guys may be living it up and laughing it up today, but one day the judgment will come. Don't be deceived. It *will* come: weep and howl for the miseries that are coming upon you."

James illustrates the transitory nature of material possessions. He says, "Your riches are corrupted, and your garments are moth-eaten."

He is addressing the sin of hoarding our wealth, hoarding our possessions. The word "corrupted" here conveys the idea of rotting away. James says, "Your riches are rotting away." Much like today, the abundance of clothing was a sign of wealth. James says, "Your garments are moth-eaten." In essence he asks, "Why store up so much clothing in order to feed moths?" The hoarding of one's possessions raises questions of responsible stewardship.

Have you ever watched the American television show "Hoarders" or "American Pickers?" In the latter show, a couple of guys travel all over the country looking for old things to buy and resell. In their journeys they come across a lot of interesting characters, many of whom have barns chock-full of "junk." Often one of the "pickers" will find some small, obscure item amidst so much surrounding junk and make an offer to purchase it from the owner. Frequently the owners will have great difficulty parting with what they have: "Nah," they reluctantly respond, "I can't let that one go." So the item is placed back down among the vast sea of surrounding clutter.

Many of us watching shows like that shake our heads in disbelief. But what about us? Are we guilty of hoarding? How much clutter fills our dressers, our closets, our attics, or our basements? How many of us have to rent a storage facility to store more "stuff?" If so, shouldn't the fact that we actually *pay* someone monthly to keep our "stuff" give us pause? We are paying for something to be locked up and never used!

Once again, James echoes teachings of his half-brother, Jesus:

> Do not lay up for yourselves treasures on earth, where moth and rust destroy and where thieves break in and steal; but lay up for yourselves treasures in heaven, where neither moth nor rust destroys and where thieves do not break in and steal. For where your treasure is, there your heart will be also (Matthew 6:19-21).

James continues: "Your gold and silver are corroded, and their corrosion will be a witness against you and will eat your flesh like fire. You have heaped up treasure in the last days."

This phrase, "the last days," is a reference to judgment, judgment day. These wealthy landowners have been deceived by the immediate gratification they are receiving from their possessions. It is as though their possessions and their lives will go on forever. James addresses that deception with sobering truth.

While gold and silver do not actually corrode, James is not talking so much about the physical properties of precious metals as he is talking about the failure of these possessions to survive the day of judgment. On that day much that seemed so valuable and important will be worthless and unimportant.

And, while the popular truism about money is helpful: "You can't take it with you," there is one sense in which our riches may be "present" after we die. James teaches that some of us may see those riches again when they "witness against us" on the day of judgment. It's a frightening thing to imagine that our possessions may appear on the witness stand before the Lord as if to say, "I am his god. He did not worship You. He worshiped me."

Money may Deceive us. Secondly:

Money may Destroy us

Where James warns the wealthy that riches "will eat their flesh like fire" he's warning what will happen if money becomes their god. Money cannot save us from the fires of judgment. Money has the potential, then, to destroy us. He adds: Indeed the wages of the laborers who mowed your fields, which you kept back by fraud, cry out; and the cries of the reapers have reached the ears of the Lord of Sabaoth."

Apparently these greedy landowners were treating their laborers unjustly. Day laborers were common in New Testament times. You'll recall where Jesus said that when we pray we our to say, "Give us this day our daily bread (Matthew 6:11)," which suggests many folks worked for the bread they would receive that very day. They labored during the day—usually in fields—and would be paid at the end of the day for their labor.

The Old Testament was very specific in commanding that day laborers be treated justly, whether they were believers or unbelievers:

> You shall not oppress a hired servant who is poor and needy, whether one of your brethren or one of the aliens who is in your land within your gates.
> Each day you shall give him his wages, and not let the sun go down on it, for he is poor and has set his heart on it; lest he cry out against you to the Lord, and it be sin to you (Deuteronomy 24:14-15).

Failure to pay a man his wages at the end of the day was a sin. This is the sin addressed by James in this text. The wealthy landowners held back the wages ("kept back by fraud") rightly due to the reapers, those who had "mowed (their) fields."

As a result James says "the cries of the reapers have reached the ears of the Lord of Sabaoth." This phrase means "the Lord of hosts," or, "the Lord of the heavenly armies." It's a title that stresses God's sovereignty. God sees all things, hears all things, knows all things, and controls all things. He knows what's going on with these wealthy landowners and He will not remain silent.

Again James uses picturesque language to describe the judgment. He says that the unpaid wages "cry out." It is as if the money that these greedy landowners had kept in their closets or underneath their mattresses begins to speak, or to cry out: "Unjust! Unjust! Pay the day laborer!"

And while the rich landowners apparently are deaf to the cry of this money, nothing is wrong with God's hearing. God hears the cry. The sovereign God who is just and one day will render a final, complete, and just judgment—He hears all things.

James goes on to suggest that these greedy, wealthy landowners were acting in ways that led to the deaths of those who were oppressed. The righteous laborers were in no position to resist and consequently died at the hands of the rich: "You have condemned, you have murdered the just; he does not resist you."

Ironically, however, it is the rich landowners who are soon approaching their own doom. James puts it this way: "You have lived on the earth in pleasure and luxury; you have fattened your hearts as in a day of slaughter."

During a recent summer I was visiting some of my family who live in Western Nebraska. They are true Americans, farmers for decades in the heartland. We would sit down to breakfast or dinner and I would say something like, "This sausage is really good." And they'd say, "Well, that's Janelle's pig." Or we'd sit down at dinner and I'd say, "These steaks look good" and they'd say, "Yep, that's Kerry's cow." This was a bit unusual for me as I was in the habit of buying sausage and steaks at the local grocery.

But think of it: you drive past fields of cattle and you nearly always see them eating. They're just lying around and eating. Eating, eating, eating. It seems like a pretty good life, right?! Of course what those cattle do not know is that they are eating—

to be eaten! They don't know that this "life of luxury" is leading them to a certain doom. They are being fattened for the day of slaughter.

This is precisely what James says is happening to the self-indulgent rich: "You have lived on the earth in pleasure and luxury; you have fattened your hearts as in a day of slaughter."

Do you see the danger of allowing riches to become your god? Our riches can deceive us into thinking that life is merely about self-indulgence, ease, buying, or hoarding. And we may obtain more riches by oppressing others. Like a grazing cow, we just munch away, all the while fattening ourselves for the slaughter —the judgment to come.

This warning is not just for "other people" we believe to be rich. This passage is for every single one of us, no matter the level of our income. Frankly, most of us living in America are rich in terms of history and geography. We are far more wealthy than generations before us and far wealthier than many folks living across the globe.

By way of application, let me suggest three actions to take in response to James' warning.

Be Wise: Live with Eternity in View

Recall what James said at the end of chapter 4: "What is your life? It is even a vapor that appears for a little time and then vanishes away. You ought to say, "If the Lord wills, we shall live... (James 4:14-15)."

Live with eternity in view. Never forget that this world is not your final home. Don't be deceived by riches—or anything else. The day of judgment will come when we will give an accounting of whether we have bowed before Jesus Christ and followed Him as Lord. Don't allow riches to be your god.

The Apostle Paul also warns what will happen if money is our god. He says:

> But those who desire to be rich fall into temptation and a snare, and into many foolish and harmful lusts which drown men in destruction and perdition. For the love of money is a root of all kinds of evil, for which some have strayed from the faith in their greediness, and pierced themselves through with many sorrows (1 Timothy 6:9-10).

Live with eternity in view. Money comes and goes. Solomon wisely advises: "Cast but a glance at riches, and they are gone, for they will surely sprout wings and fly off to the sky like an eagle (Proverbs 23:5)."

So live with eternity in view. Live for Jesus. Know that true wealth is found in Him. As the Apostle Paul says of Christ: "Though He was rich, yet for your sakes He became poor, that you through His poverty might become rich (2 Corinthians 8:9)."

True wealth is found in Christ. Love of money is but a cheap substitute for love of Christ. Love Christ, really love Him, re-calling what He has done for you. Think of Him throughout the day, mediate upon His works on your behalf:

Living, He loved me
Dying, He saved me
Buried, He carried my sins far away
Rising, He justified freely forever
One day He's coming
Oh glorious day![27]

Be wise: live with eternity in view. Second action:

Be Content: Enjoy what You Have

At the beginning of our study we noted that being wealthy is not a sin, in and of itself. What is wrong is a wealthy person's sinful attitude toward wealth. In the same way, however, a poor person can have a sinful attitude toward wealth.

JC Ryle observes with his inimitable simplicity: "We may love money without having it, just as we may have money without loving it."[28]

In the oft-quoted platitude: Money is not the problem, *love* of money is the problem.

Be content: enjoy what you have. Don't live beyond your means. Third action:

Be Generous: Give to Bless Others

Rather than hoarding, give. Rather than collecting, give away. Be a good steward. Save for the future.

In a sermon on tithing, John Piper challenges Christians to give beyond the traditional tithe (10 percent). He argues:

> My own conviction is that most…Americans who merely tithe are robbing God. In a world where 10,000 people a day starve to death and many more than that are perishing in unbelief the question is not, "What percentage must I give?" but, "How much dare I spend on myself?"[29]

Good question. Christian Author Randy Alcorn seems to agree. He writes: "God prospers me not to raise my standard of living but to raise my standard of giving."[30]

Be generous: give to bless others.

What About You?

How is James' teaching similar to Jesus' parable of the "rich fool" in Luke 12:13-21?

What is your opinion on tithing? How much do you give and why?

Of Jesus Paul said, "Though He was rich, yet for your sakes He became poor, that you through His poverty might become rich

(2 Corinthians 8:9)." What exactly does that mean? How does it apply to you?

❊ ❊ ❊

Chapter 20: Be Patient
(James 5:7-11)

7 Therefore be patient, brethren, until the coming of the Lord. See how the farmer waits for the precious fruit of the earth, waiting patiently for it until it receives the early and latter rain.

8 You also be patient. Establish your hearts, for the coming of the Lord is at hand.

9 Do not grumble against one another, brethren, lest you be condemned. Behold, the Judge is standing at the door!

10 My brethren, take the prophets, who spoke in the name of the Lord, as an example of suffering and patience.

11 Indeed we count them blessed who endure. You have heard of the perseverance of Job and seen the end intended by the Lord—that the Lord is very compassionate and merciful.

Because James begins this passage with the word "Therefore," a word that suggests he means, "In light of what I have just said," we understand that James is providing information that comes on the heels of what was previously written.

We recall from our last study that James addressed an injustice occurring in the areas surrounding Jerusalem and beyond, specifically the matter of wealthy landowners working their farmhands but not paying them properly. Greedy businessmen were holding on to the wages they should have been paying to those under their employ.

We imagine how those cheated workers must have felt. Surely they wondered how long this injustice would continue. Like any other trial or difficulty in life, we often wonder why it seems to go unnoticed by society—or unchecked by God. We may even wonder whether God is aware of this circumstance or why He doesn't seem to be doing anything about it.

James teaches what Christians are to do when they find themselves in the throes of injustice. In short, he instructs them to remember that the Lord is coming again. And to remember that when He comes He will right all wrongs. James says, "Be patient, brethren, until the coming of the Lord." He describes the Lord's coming as imminent: "The coming of the Lord is at hand," and "the Judge is standing at the door!"

The Lord's second coming is the next "big thing" God has planned. You might think of it as the next major event He has "calendared." Many of us have planners or calendars, or we keep a list of tasks, or even a "to do list." We list the routine things we do every day and then there is the separate list of bigger tasks, larger, more important tasks we aim to attack.

If we think of God this way and were to imagine that He kept a calendar, and were we able to look at His "to do list" of big tasks, we would find just one item remaining on His list. We would see previous tasks crossed through, finished tasks such as creation, fall, Christ's first coming and redemption. Then there would be that remaining item, the unfinished task: "Second Coming." There would be no line through it because, of course, it has yet to occur!

The second coming of Christ is God's next "big thing" that He has planned. In God's sovereign, providential working through history, we are they who live between Christ's first and second comings. So while God is at work in all events, including the daily things that happen at all times, we look forward to the next "big thing" God will do in fulfillment of His overarching plan for humankind. We look forward to Christ's return.

It is helpful to think this way every day and especially helpful to think this way when we find ourselves in difficult circumstances. Especially when we suffer injustices, James encourages us to "be patient," to wait patiently for that future time when Christ returns and God settles the score.

This takes us to the first practical action that surfaces from these verses:

Look for the Savior, that you may Endure

The way we can move forward when difficulties come is by looking up and watching for the Savior. By this, I mean we are to have a heart attitude and disposition that looks beyond the present difficulty. We anticipate the fulfillment of a greater plan that God is working out. Doing this results in an ability to endure.

James teaches that just as a farmer waits patiently for the coming of rain so should the Christian wait patiently for the coming of Christ.

I'm not a farmer, but I know how important water is to farming. When I visited my farming cousins I mentioned in a previous chapter, they took me to an aqueduct built by a relative. He had been one of the homesteaders who settled that dry, western area of Nebraska. Of course water is essential for the growing of crops.

In James' day—and throughout the Old and New Testaments—

we see Palestinian farmers dependent upon two seasons of rain, the "early" and "latter" rains. The early rain was what God sent in the fall, the rain that occurred just after sowing the fields. The latter rain came the following spring just before the harvest time.

Farmers had to wait patiently for the rain. They could not speed up this process! They had to just wait upon the Lord. They had to believe that He was going to do something and that the timing would be right.

So James says this is precisely the way you and I are to live when we face injustices and difficulties. Whatever our trials and tribulations, we wait upon the Lord. We must believe He will do something and His help will come at just the right time.

Interestingly James comes full circle, providing "bookends" to his letter. In this last chapter he is tying the theme of perseverance to that same theme in the opening of his letter. Recall what he wrote at the beginning of the first chapter:

> My brethren, count it all joy when you fall into various trials, knowing that the testing of your faith produces patience. But let patience have its perfect work, that you may be perfect and complete, lacking nothing (James 1:2-4).

Though the words are different, James is calling for the same kind of patience here in the last chapter. God works through our hardships, difficulties, and injustices to produce a steadfastness, a patient endurance, an ability to stand firm and strong. God conforms us to Christlikeness through our hardships and develops in us the virtue of endurance.

Our role is to look up, to look for the Savior that we may endure. It's much as Paul teaches in his letters, teaching us to look to the future that we may find encouragement. To the church in Rome, for example, he says: "For I consider that the sufferings of this present time are not worthy to be compared with the glory which shall be revealed in us (Romans 8:18)," and to the church in Galatia he writes: "And let us not grow weary while doing good, for in due season we shall reap if we do not lose heart (Galatians 6:9)."

James says, "You also be patient. Establish your hearts, for the coming of the Lord is at hand."

The phrase "Establish your hearts" is a call for Christians to be strong, to shore up their faith, to have a backbone and strengthen their inner resolve to stand in the face of injustices. It's a call for courage, conviction, and commitment in times of adversity.

And again, note the key to this: it is not that we just sort of "drum up" this resolve, but rather that we find strength in the truth, the fact of the coming of the Lord. James says, "Establish your hearts, for the coming of the Lord is at hand." In other words, "Here's how to prop up your heart, here's how to stand in the face of persecution and adversity: remember that the Lord is coming and He could come today."

Similar encouragements to look for the Savior that we may endure are found in other places in the New Testament:

"The night is far spent, the day is at hand. Therefore let us cast off the works of darkness, and let us put on the armor of light (Romans 13:12)."

"Let us not forsake the assembling of ourselves together, as is the manner of some, but exhort one another, and so much the more as we see the Day approaching (Hebrews 10:25)."

"But the end of all things is at hand; therefore be serious and watchful in your prayers (1 Peter 4:7)."

Be patient. Establish your hearts, for the coming of the Lord is at hand. The idea is to persevere, to not quit, to keep moving. So as you wait patiently, look for the Savior that you may endure. Secondly, as you wait patiently:

Look to your Speech, that you may Edify

The idea here is that when we go through hardships and difficulties we must watch our mouths. When facing persecution or battling difficulties we may find ourselves grumbling or complaining. When things don't go our way we are tempted to lash out and take out our frustrations on others. James warns: "Do not grumble against one another, brethren, lest you be condemned. Behold, the Judge is standing at the door!"

James seems to understand our propensity for taking out our frustrations upon others. The very reason he is teaching patience is because of our immediate fallen reaction to become impatient. Growing increasingly impatient with God, Christians may begin taking out their frustrations on each other. So James says, "Do not grumble against one another, brethren."

The problem is not with "one another." This is nearly always helpful to remember in our dealings with others. When a person lashes out at you, you are usually not the problem. Don't take it personally. Frequently there is something else going on in that person's life and you just happen to be the nearest target. Have the wisdom to remember this the next time someone unfairly criticizes you or grumbles against you.

So James warns against lashing out when it seems that God's promises to address injustices are taking too long to be fulfilled. Don't be impatient. James adds that if we fail to be patient we will "be condemned." We will be found at fault by the Lord.

James adds: "Behold, the Judge is standing at the door!" In other words the Lord is right outside, standing at the door, and He's not going to knock first. He's just going to fling the door open suddenly and come in. It's that sudden.

Now we may think, "Well, it's been a long time since Christ's first coming. Shouldn't He have come by now? Didn't the early

Christians live as though they believed He would come soon?" And the answer is yes, the early Christians lived as though they believed He would come soon. It's the same way Christians should live today—as though they believe He will come soon.

Peter reminds us in his second letter in 2 Peter 3:9, "The Lord is not slack (or slow) concerning His promise, as some count slackness, but is long-suffering toward us, not willing that any should perish but that all should come to repentance."

In other words, if it seems like the Lord is delaying His coming, remember His love for mankind. He is "long-suffering... not willing that any should perish but that all should come to repentance," that all would be ready when He *does* come—whether by coming to us or by calling us home to Himself.

Remember that Jesus warns in Matthew's Gospel: "Be ready, for the Son of Man is coming at an hour you do not expect (Matthew 24:44)," and "Watch therefore, for you know neither the day nor the hour in which the Son of Man is coming (Matthew 25:13)."

If He came today, would you be ready? What if He calls you away in death, will you be ready? That too could happen suddenly. He could either come or call us to Himself. Will you be ready to face Him?

To us it may seem like a long time between Christ's first and second comings but remember in that same passage from 2 Peter that Peter reminds us "with the Lord one day is as a thousand years, and a thousand years as one day (2 Peter 3:8)." God works according to His own timetable.

Jesus Himself hints that there will be a long interval between His first and second comings such as in Matthew 25 in the parable of the talents: "After *a long time* the lord of those servants came and settled accounts with them (Matthew 25:19; emphasis added)."

So be patient. The Lord is coming again. Don't grow impatient and start lashing out at one another. Look for the Savior and look to your speech; watch for your Lord and watch your mouth. Thirdly, as you wait patiently:

Look at the Scriptures, that you may be Encouraged

James now encourages Christians by reminding them that in the Scriptures they will find godly examples of those who persevered through times of persecution, injustice, and adversity: "My brethren, take the prophets, who spoke in the name of the Lord, as an example of suffering and patience."

It is as though James were saying, "Just open your Bibles and you will read throughout the Old Testament about the prophets who persevered through times of hardship. They are good examples to you of how to move forward, to keep going when you suffer."

And this is true, isn't it? We do better when we find that others have experienced what we are experiencing and discover that they got through it okay. It really encourages us. So James says just read the Scriptures and you will be encouraged by the examples of prophets who persevered during hardships snd difficulties.

The writer of Hebrews seems to encourage us this way by reminding us of the many Old Testament heroes who persevered under hardship. He writes:

[Some] were tortured, not accepting deliverance, that they might obtain a better resurrection. Still others had trial of mockings and scourgings, yes, and of chains and imprisonment. They were stoned, they were sawn in two, were tempted, were slain with the sword. They wandered about in sheepskins and goatskins, being destitute, afflicted, tormented—of whom the world was not worthy. They wandered in deserts and mountains, in dens and caves of the earth (Hebrews 11:35-38).

James means to encourage Christians. In essence, he is saying: "Hey if you want to be encouraged when you're going through trials and hardships, read the Bible. Look to the Scriptures and find encouragement."

Do you read the Bible regularly? You can't be encouraged if you don't read it. James continues: "Indeed we count them blessed who endure…"

That's true. "We count them blessed who endure." Those who endure receive the prize at the end of the sufferings. To quote the Apostle Paul again: "For I consider that the sufferings of this present time are not worthy to be compared with the glory which shall be revealed in us (Romans 8:18)."

Finally, James provides Job as the quintessential example of persevering during times of trials and affliction: "Indeed we count them blessed who endure. You have heard of the perseverance of Job and seen the end intended by the Lord—that the Lord is very compassionate and merciful."

We often speak of the "patience of Job," but the word "perseverance" is better. Truth is, Job occasionally comes across as a bit *impatient* (as we typically understand the term) and who can blame him? He lost all of his children, he lost his home, he lost his stuff, and then he's covered in boils. It's so bad that Job's wife does what James warns against in verse 9. She grumbles and says, "Job, why don't you just curse God and die?"—just the kind of encouragement he needed, right?!

But James reminds us that God had a sovereign plan He was working in and through Job's circumstances. James says, "You and I can see the end—(the word means 'purpose')—the end intended by the Lord."

God had a purpose He was working out in the life of Job. And James gives us something of that purpose in verse 11, that we may see that "the Lord is very compassionate and merciful."

God blesses Job in the end with twice as much as he had before. Job didn't know that God would do this back at the beginning of the ordeal. He could only persevere during the "question marks" of his life. He persevered through the afflictions and God honored his faithfulness.

Matthew Henry says, "The best way to bear afflictions is to look to the end of them."[31]

Remember that God is sovereign and that He is working out an "end," a purpose, and that His purpose will be good and right. Never forget that. He is always, as James says at the end of verse 11, "very compassionate and merciful."

Be patient. Don't quit on God! After all, He doesn't quit on us.

What About You?

Why do you think the Lord has delayed His second coming?

Why do you think the Lord permits so much injustice?

Does reading in the Bible about the oppression of others encourage you? Why or why not?

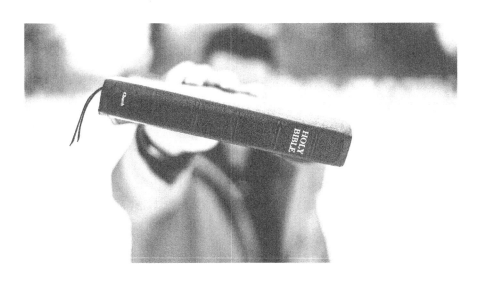

Chapter 21: I Swear On The Bible!
(James 5:12)

12 But above all, my brethren, do not swear, either by heaven or by earth or with any other oath. But let your "Yes" be "Yes," and your "No," "No," lest you fall into judgment.

Thanks to my younger son, nearly every time I read this verse I am reminded of a classic scene in an episode of "The Three Stooges." In the 1936 episode, "Disorder in the Court," Curly is being sworn-in to testify as a key witness to a murder trial. There is an extensive back-and-forth between the bailiff and Curly as the bailiff tries his level best to get Curly —who is also holding a cane—to take off his hat, place his left hand on the Bible, and raise his right hand.

Curly just can't seem to figure out how to do all three actions at once. The bailiff becomes greatly agitated and the problem escalates when the exasperated bailiff, in an effort to end the ordeal as swiftly as possible, hurriedly rattles off the familiar question: "Do you swear to tell the truth, the whole truth, and noting but the truth?" Curly can't understand the bailiff's speedy question so the drollery continues for quite some time before Curly is finally "sworn-in."

It really is a funny spectacle! But goofball antics of this scene notwithstanding, what place does James' teaching in verse 12 have in today's court of law? Does he forbid the Christian's taking an oath to provide testimony? Is it wrong for Christians to place their hand upon a Bible and swear an oath of office? There are some who think so. They read this verse along with statements made by our Lord Jesus and conclude that they cannot, in good conscience, swear to take an oath of any kind.

On surface level, James' words certainly seem to forbid such oath-taking. At the same time, given the wider scope of scriptural teaching, I do not think the Bible forbids wholesale the practice of taking oaths.

Before we consider precisely what James is teaching here, we may feel that this verse seems a bit out of place. How does this seemingly random verse fit in to the overall context of James' letter?

If there is one thing we've learned about James it is that he has much to say about the use and misuse of our tongues. While chapter 3 stands out as the primary chapter on misuse of the tongue, James' teaching on this subject begins as early as the first chapter where he cautions against one's "saying" he is tempted by God (James 1:13).

Recall that he warned in the same chapter, "If anyone among you thinks he is religious, and does not bridle his tongue but deceives his own heart, this one's religion is useless (James 1:26)."

You'll also remember that in Chapter 2 James warns against our "saying" to the poor and shabbily dressed worshiper, "You stand over there (James 2:3)" and he rebukes us for ever "saying" a Christian can have faith without works (James 2:12).

Then there is that extensive and exhaustive treatment of the tongue in chapter 3, verses 1 through 12. James warns that our tongues are a fire, a world of iniquity (James 3:6) and, "an unruly evil, full of deadly poison (James 3:8)."

In chapter 4 he warns, "Do not speak evil of one another, brethren. He who speaks evil of a brother...speaks evil of the law and judges the law (James 4:11)."

And in our previous study of the opening verses of chapter 5 (the verses immediately preceding our text), we read where James warns—in the context of injustice—"Do not grumble against one another, brethren, lest you be condemned (James 5:9)."

This last warning (verse 9) is especially helpful in providing context for verse 12. It is often when we go through trials, temptations, and injustices that we are especially vulnerable and most likely to say things we will later regret.

Consider Peter's behavior on the night Jesus was betrayed. Peter was rather "oath-like" in his verbal stand for Christ. Earlier in the evening he had boasted, "Even if all are made to stumble because of You, I will never be made to stumble (Matthew 26:33)." But of course, Peter himself ended up "stumbling," abandoning Jesus. Later, when under pressure to reveal himself as a follower of Christ, Peter thrice denied his Lord, swearing: "I do not know the Man (Matthew 26:69-75)!"

Perhaps it is this kind of behavior foremost in James' thinking when he writes verse 12. We cannot say for certain, but we do know that the misuse of our words is a prominent theme in this letter.

Having established the immediate context of verse 12, let us consider a few other passages where oaths are mentioned in the Bible.

It was not uncommon in New Testament times to use oaths in a self-serving way, a means by which to be evasive or avoid personal responsibility. An oath might be taken not so much to bind one to a commitment, but rather as the means by which to get out of one.

For example in Matthew's Gospel, Jesus warns:

> Woe to you, blind guides, who say, 'Whoever swears by the temple, it is nothing; but whoever swears by the gold of the temple, he is obliged to perform it.' Fools and blind! For which is greater, the gold or the temple that sanctifies the gold (Matthew 23:16-17)?

In addition to addressing the creation of superficial distinctions in the law, Jesus teaches that it is always wrong to use an oath to get out of one's word.

Oaths used this way often provided a "loophole" to one's pledge, an "escape hatch" to get out of a commitment. We may imagine a person saying something like, "Look I know I promised. I know I gave you my word, but you need to remember that I swore only by the *temple*, not by the *gold* of the temple! So I am not obliged to keep my promise."

This is not too dissimilar from the oaths many of us took on the playground as small children. We would "promise" to do some such thing, but behind our backs we crossed our fingers. We believed that if we had our fingers crossed, then our oath was not binding. And if we really meant to keep our word we would say something like: "Cross my heart and hope to die, stick a needle in my eye (whatever *that* means!)."

Jesus also addresses the danger of attempting to strengthen our words by swearing oaths. In the Sermon on the Mount, He says:

> Again you have heard that it was said to those of old, "You shall not swear falsely, but shall perform your oaths to the Lord." But I say to you, do not swear at all: neither by heaven, for it is God's throne; nor by the earth, for it is His footstool; nor by Jerusalem, for it is the city of the great King. Nor shall

you swear by your head, because you cannot make one hair white or black. But let your "Yes" be "Yes," and your "No," "No." For whatever is more than these is from the evil one (Matthew 5:33-37).

This particular matter of trying to strengthen one's words by adding an oath seems to be at the center of what James forbids in verse 12. The idea is, "Don't seek to strengthen or enforce your words by adding an oath to them. Just keep your word!"

At the same time, it seems clear that the Bible does not entirely forbid the practice of taking oaths.

Jesus Himself took an oath. During His trial, the high priest looked at Jesus and said, "I charge You under oath by the Living God, are You the son of God?" And Jesus replied, under oath, "Yes, I am; it is as you say (Matthew 26:63-64)."

Paul's second letter to the Church at Corinth records an "oath like" manner of speaking: "Moreover I call God as witness against my soul, that to spare you I came no more to Corinth (2 Corinthians 1:23; *cf*. Galatians 1:20; Philippians 1:8)."

God the Father took an oath when making His covenant with Abraham. According to the writer of Hebrews: "When God made his promise to Abraham, since there was no one greater for him to swear by, he swore by himself (Hebrews 6:13)."

So when we compare Scripture with Scripture it is hard to conclude that the Bible strictly forbids the taking of all oaths, without exception.

On the contrary it would seem that, given man's fallen nature, oaths would be helpful in situations such as a court of law. It is precisely because we are sinners, liars at heart, that oaths have proved helpful in ascertaining the truth. Given man's propensity for trying to find loopholes, a solemn ceremony wherein one is formally bound to tell the truth seems especially needful in modern civilization.

Think about it: Why do we require the placing of one's hand on the Bible anyway? In other words, if one has to place his or her hand on the Bible in order to guarantee that he or she is *now* going to be telling the truth, what does this say about the way a person naturally goes about speaking and behaving when he or she is *not* placing a hand upon the Bible?

It is as though we are saying, "Oh, but I mean it now, you see. After all, I am placing my hand upon the Bible!" Or better: "I will place my hand upon a *stack* of bibles!"

This reasoning sounds very much like the Pharisee who says: "I swear not merely by the *temple*, but by the *gold* of the temple!"

So while the custom of taking an oath such as in a court of law may be permissible in our day, a Christian should never feel the need to strengthen or enforce his words by the taking of an oath. This seems to be more what James is after here in verse 12:

"But above all, my brethren, do not swear, either by heaven or by earth or with any other oath. But let your "Yes" be "Yes," and your "No," "No," lest you fall into judgment.

In essence, James is saying, "Look, don't be like some unbeliever who has to enforce his words with an oath. You don't place your hand on the Bible only when you mean it because, as a Christian, your hand is *always* on the Bible."[32]

There are No Levels of Truthfulness

For the Christian there are no levels of truthfulness. We do not reason: "Well this is one level of truth here, and then there is this little bit of "gray area" here, so I can tell the whole truth here and fudge a little there."

Christians are expected to be completely truthful at all times. Placing your hand on the Bible doesn't suddenly make you a truth-teller. Placing your hand on the Bible, for the Christian, is really of no consequence because the true Christian always tells the truth.

God is your Judge (*cf.* James 5:9) and you are always "under oath." Always! You are always "sworn in."

There are no levels of truthfulness to your employer, to your clients, to your co-worker, to your parents, to your children, or to your spouse. Let your "Yes" be "Yes" and your "No," "No." Be a person of your word. Tell the truth every time. Don't fudge. Don't look for the loophole.

There are No Levels of Integrity

Christians will not fudge the truth, nor compromise their morality, nor cheapen their integrity. They endeavor to walk not in worldliness, but in holiness.

So there are no levels of integrity in your marriage. You said to your spouse, "I do." There was no qualification to that commitment. You said, "Yes" so let your "Yes" be "Yes."

You said, "For richer or for poorer, for sickness and in health, for the good times, and the bad times, too."

Those who know us should regard us as those who always tell the truth. We are a people "set apart" from the average person. And our motivation for always telling the truth comes from God's truthfulness to us. His "Yes" can be taken to the bank.

Imagine If God changed His "Yes" to No!" God has said wonderful things such as, "The one who comes to Me I will by no means cast out (John 6:37)" or, "If anyone thirsts, let him come to Me and drink (John 7:37)." Or consider this classic promise: "Though your sins are like scarlet, they shall be as white as snow; though they are red like crimson, they shall be as wool (Isaiah 1:18)."

So imagine if God were to say to you, "Look, I didn't really mean *you*. I didn't really mean *all* of what I said. I wasn't talking about forgiving *that* sin!"

Here is the supreme motivator for our own faithfulness: God's faithfulness to us. God's faithfulness to us motivates our faithfulness to Him and our faithfulness to others.

What About You?

Are you comfortable taking an oath in a court of law? Why or why not? Be sure to use Scripture to support your answer.

How does secular society view telling the truth? Why do you think that is?

Are you known as a person of your word?

❋ ❋ ❋

Chapter 22: Talking to God
(James 5:13-15)

13 Is anyone among you suffering? Let him pray. Is anyone cheerful? Let him sing psalms.
14 Is anyone among you sick? Let him call for the elders of the church, and let them pray over him, anointing him with oil in the name of the Lord.
15 And the prayer of faith will save the sick, and the Lord will raise him up. And if he has committed sins, he will be forgiven.

Several years ago a disc in my back herniated, causing sudden compression on a couple of nerves, resulting in intense, debilitating pain. I had often had back issues, but this was really painful. I hurt from my lower back all the way down my leg and into my big toe! A couple doctor visits later, I was told by a physician that he could perform a procedure that would take care of the pain. It was a minimally invasive surgery and the doctor assured me he had performed the procedure hundreds of times. It sounded good and I knew I couldn't continue taking pain medication so I allowed him to schedule the procedure.

Before the day came, however, I was beginning to have second thoughts. After all, who really wants to have someone cut on him if he can avoid it? More importantly, I had not really prayed about healing and began thinking that it was foolish for me to go through with a surgical procedure without first praying, asking God to heal me.

To make a long story short, I cancelled the operation and asked God to heal me of the back pain. Admittedly, I am not the sort of person who routinely asks for healing, and am naturally skeptical of sensational "healing stories." But I really believed God was testing me in an effort to strengthen my faith.

A couple days later I shared with my pastoral staff what was going on and asked them if they would do as James teaches in this text. They agreed and gathered around me and laid hands on me. We prayed together, asking God to heal my back.

That was seven years ago and I have not had any recurring issues. Occasionally, I will feel a little tingling in my big toe—it doesn't hurt, but I'll notice it every once in a while. When I do, I take it as a gentle reminder that it was God who healed me of my back pain.

I really believe God worked this way to get me to talk with Him. As I have said, it is not as though this sort of thing happens to me all the time—it doesn't. I don't have a lot of "moving testimonies" about the power of God's healing in my life. I just believe that in this case God was testing me to strengthen my faith, drawing me to Himself so that I would talk to Him, asking Him for healing.

It is often said that prayer is simply "taking" to God. We simply go to Him, taking our burdens to Him, asking for His help. It's like the hymn:

What a privilege to carry
Everything to God in prayer!

Have we trials and temptations?
Is there trouble anywhere?

Are we weak and heavy-laden,
Cumbered with a load of care?
Precious Savior, still our refuge—
Take it to the Lord in prayer.[33]

In this passage, James provides three specific circumstances where Christians are to pray.

Talk to God when Suffering

James opens the passage this way: "Is anyone among you suffering? Let him pray." That's pretty simple and straightforward. If you are suffering, pray! Talk to God.

It makes sense to go to God because He is the One who made us and knows us. If you own a Mac computer and your computer breaks down, you don't talk to the Windows guy, you talk to the Apple guy because Apple is the one who made it and knows it.

So where do you go when *you* "break down?" Go to the One who made you and knows you. Talk to God.

Heres an important qualifier: James does *not* say that you are guaranteed to stop suffering when you go to God. He does not teach that. Suffering through trials is often a good thing for Christians because it helps them grow. You'll recall that truth from the opening verses of the letter:

My brethren, count it all joy when you fall into various trials, knowing that the testing of your faith produces patience (or endurance). But let endurance have its perfect work, that you may be perfect and complete, lacking nothing. (James 1:2-4).

Suffering is a means God often uses in the Christian's life to make the Christian more like Jesus. God may work through our suffering to remove unhelpful impurities in our lives; worldliness, for example.

Talk to God when suffering. As someone taught me years ago: when you suffer try not to ask God, "Why?" but rather ask Him, "What?" As in, "What are you teaching me, God? What are you trying to show me through my suffering? What lessons would you like me to learn? What are you doing right now to make me more like Jesus?"

Talk to God when suffering. Secondly:

Talk to God when Singing

I've worded this point by stressing the content of its application. The text actually reads: "Is anyone cheerful? Let him sing psalms." I am stressing the *content* of our singing, that we are—in song—talking to God.

We talk to God when suffering and we are also to talk to God when *not* suffering. We talk to God not just in the *absence* of cheer, but also in the *presence* of cheer. James says, "Is anyone cheerful? Let him sing psalms."

When you're happy, sing! But what exactly is James encouraging us to sing? Is he calling for us to simply sing with no regard for the content of our words? Or is he calling for something else?

Specifically James says, "Is anyone cheerful, let him sing *psalms*." The New King James is helpful here because most of the modern translations have simply, "Let him sing praise," or "praises," which might suggest generic singing regardless of the content.

But the word for praise is the word "psalms," like the psalms of the Old Testament, words of praise to the One True and Living God. Greek scholar A.T. Robertson says this word "psalms" means "to sing praise to God whether with instrument or without."[34]

So James is talking about our singing *to God* as the object of our praise. "Is anyone cheerful? Let him sing psalms," songs of praise to God. Perhaps we will find ourselves singing the familiar doxology: "Praise God From Whom All Blessings Flow." Or maybe we will simply sing the contemplative chorus: "Alleluia," which means, of course, "Praise the Lord."

God loves to hear His children praise Him in song! How important it is for us all to sing. The corporate worship service is not a performance by the choir or the praise team. The choir and the praise team *lead* in worship. We are *all* to be worshiping. Words to every song should be printed or projected where all can see the content of the lyrical text. The words are meant to be spoken by all, whether silently or aloud. After all, we gather to praise Him!

And the same is true when we are in private worship, driving in our cars or walking outside, or kneeling in prayer. We praise the Lord in song.

In our initial reading of verse 13, we may find ourselves more easily drawn to the first part of the verse: "Is anyone among you *suffering*? Let him pray" than the second part: "Is anyone *cheerful*? Let him sing psalms."

Ironically, it is often the second part of the verse that is the harder thing to do. Personally I find that when things are going bad, it's easier and more natural to talk to God than when things are going well. When things are going really well, I find it harder to remember God. It's so easy to neglect Him.

When it's dark and we are hurting, we're more inclined to go to God. And too often we do so in anger: "Why are You doing this to me?!" Yet, when it's not dark and we are not suffering, when the sun is shining and everything feels good, in those moments it is frightfully easy to forget God. We must never forget James' teaching in the opening chapter: "Every good and perfect gift comes from above (James 1:17)."

We talk to God not just in the *absence* of cheer, but in the *presence* of cheer. Worship is ongoing. We ought always to be talking to God, talking to God when suffering and talking to God when singing.

Talk to God when Sick

James provides now a third occasion for our talking to God. He writes:

> Is anyone among you sick? Let him call for the elders of the church, and let them pray over him, anointing him with oil in the name of the Lord. And the prayer of faith will save the sick, and the Lord will raise him up. And if he has committed sins, he will be forgiven.

The text assumes a kind of sickness that requires special prayer. This is a physical sickness that seems to imply one is perhaps bedridden as a result of the physical ailment—though we need not restrict the application to such a situation, nor be dogmatic here in our interpretation.

These two verses are rather unique in their placement within the wider span of Scripture. One is hard-pressed to locate another passage similar to this text. Perhaps this is one reason why commentators differ widely on their interpretation of the passage.

This should give us pause as we study the text and engender humility in our conclusions. Perhaps some of us were told years ago what these verses meant or we have read our favorite commentary and happily agree with the author. In any case, we should always be willing to have our "pre-understandings" challenged by careful scrutiny of the Word.

There are some truths in the Bible that are manifestly clear. Jesus Christ, for example, is the only way to be saved. The Bible is very clear on that. It is a primary teaching. But there are many secondary or tertiary teachings that are not as clear and therefore must be held in greater tension as we seek to understand their meanings.

Years ago I was helped by learning a general rule of Bible study: "If the plain sense makes sense, seek no other sense." For example, if a simple, straightforward meaning of the text unfolds before us, then there is no reason to look for metaphor or mystery. Some things are meant to be taken at face value, pure and simple. Let us try to apply that rule as we study these two verses.

James writes, "Is anyone among you sick? Let him call for the elders of the church, and let them pray over him, anointing him with oil in the name of the Lord."

Taken in a straightforward manner, James' teaching is clear and simple. If anyone in the congregation is sick, he or she is to call for the elders of the church. The elders will gather around the individual, praying over him or her, and anointing with oil in the name of the Lord.

We may imagine a person bedridden, most likely, but not necessarily. The individual is to call for the elders of the church. Let us note that carefully: it is the person himself or herself who makes the request. It is not someone acting on behalf of the sick person, though again we don't want to be too restrictive. If someone is acting on behalf of the sick individual, he or she will be certain to gain the consent of the one who is ill.

I do not believe James has in mind a "surprise visit" by a team of "faith healers" from a nearby church or ministry. We must honor the wishes of the one who is sick. If he or she is desirous, a request will be made to the elders of his or her church.

The word "elders" here is a term used interchangeably with "bishops," or "ministers" or "pastors." They all refer to the same office, pastor of a church. The New Testament seems to assume a plurality of pastors or elders in the congregation. That assumption is seen especially here in verse 14. Note the plural, "elders of the church."

At the same time, however, I do not think that a church *must* have more than one elder present in a congregation to be considered a biblical church. Frankly, I do not know how many churches would even begin were we to take the plural as requiring the presence of more than one elder in every assembly.

While there is varied opinion on the matter of church governance and elders, I do believe the New Testament teaching suggests that a plurality of elders is preferred.

It is also important, as we have previously intimated, that this verse assumes the existence of a an actual church, a congregation, as the context in which the request is made. James refers to the elders of "the church." The New Testament takes for granted that every Christian is an active member of a local church, a local fellowship of believers *among whom* each Christian worships, prays, and serves, and *to whom* each Christian is accountable.

So the person who is sick—likely bedridden—is the one to call for the elders of the church, but even here I do not think the text *requires* the presence of elders only. There may be others who have gifts for praying and healing, but James mentions elders in particular. They come and "pray over" the one who is sick. And James adds, "anointing him with oil in the name of the Lord."

I believe this phrase, "anointing him with oil," means exactly what it says. I do not think James has in mind the medicinal use of oil as in the parable of the Good Samaritan, but rather the use of oil as a symbol for the powerful work of the Holy Spirit. Especially in the early church, the Holy Spirit's coming for healing was symbolized in the anointing with oil. Mark says, for example, that Jesus'disciples "anointed with oil many that were sick and healed them (Mark 6:13)."

Of course it is not the oil that heals but, as the last part of verse 14 indicates: "the name of the Lord." The oil is not necessary for healing, but is a powerful visual reminder of the presence and work of the Holy Spirit.

And while oil is not necessary for healing, why *not* use it? Why not use the oil if, in fact, it is a powerful reminder of the wonderful work of God's Spirit? Why would the elders, ministers, and leaders *not* use oil when praying in these circumstances? If this verse is properly explained to all gathered, I find no good reason why oil should not be used.

Again it is not the oil itself that heals, but "the name of the Lord" through the prayer of faith. As James goes on to say: "And the prayer of faith will save the sick, and the Lord will raise him up. And if he has committed sins, he will be forgiven."

Before we study this phrase, "the prayer of faith," it may be helpful to review why we even have sickness in the first place.

Physical sickness originates in the Fall of Mankind in Genesis 3. When our first parents, Adam and Eve, sinned they brought death into the world. Unless Christ returns first, every one of us will die a physical death and most of us will die as a result of some kind of sickness. In a very real sense we all have a terminal disease.

Christ's atoning work on the cross redeems Christians from the finality of sickness and death. When Christ returns, His coming will eventuate in a perfect state for Christians, a place where there is no longer sorrow, sickness, nor death (Revelation 21:4).

In the meantime, as Christians await His coming, they get sick from time to time. On some occasions, God chooses to heal us through His provision of medicine, medicine coming from substances He placed in the earth at creation, which creation He called "very good." So God chooses on occasion to heal us through medicine.

At other times, God chooses us to heal through the power of prayer. These intermediate healings are, of course, temporary insofar as we will eventually get sick again or contract some other disease.

But it is important to recognize that every healing is ultimately to the credit of God. Even doctors and physicians owe their skills and talents to the God who has endowed them. While we are grateful for every secondary cause through which God works and should thank each and every person involved, God alone deserves ultimate credit for every healing. This truth is suggested even here at the end of verse 15 where James says, "and the Lord will raise him up."

It is also important to understand that every healing is something of a foretaste of that glorious final state of perfection. In a sense, every healing foreshadows the splendor and wonder of the heavenly state where doctors, medicines, and surgeries will no longer be required.

There is something else significant about this phrase, "the prayer of faith." James indicates that it is the faith of the elders, the ones doing the praying, that is effectual in the sick person's healing, not the sick person himself.

How unfortunate that many have been told that they were not healed because they lacked faith. James does not teach here that a person is healed only when he or she has enough faith. The one being healed may have great faith or weak faith. Given the state of his illness, he may barely be able to understand what is even happening at the moment.

It seems rather that the "prayer of faith" is that unique working of God within the ones doing the praying, where God gives a special sense that He is indeed going to heal. God sovereignly chooses when to bless someone with this impression, a subjective assurance of faith, a strong sense that this sickness will be healed. And God gives that assurance, on occasion, to those who are praying.

The "prayer of faith" is not guaranteed to occur in every situation. Therefore, we must guard against any notion that a person "must" be healed. Physical healing is not always God's will this side of heaven.

While we do not know exactly what Paul's "thorn in the flesh" was, many scholars believe it was a physical malady of some kind. In any case, Paul's prayer that "it might depart" was not granted (2 Corinthians 12:7-10). What is more, this apostle who frequently was an instrument of healing in the Book of Acts, was apparently powerless to help Timothy's stomach ailment (1 Timothy 5:23) and had to leave Trophimus in Miletus because he was sick (2 Timothy 4:20). Physical healing is not always God's will.

The final phrase in this verse merits some treatment. James says, "…And if he has committed sins, he will be forgiven." This phrase suggests that not all sickness is related to sin. James speaks conditionally here: "If." The word "if" suggests that what follows may not always be the case. As we noted earlier, the presence of sickness in this life is part and parcel of living in a fallen world.

There are occasions, however, where one's illness *is* tied to a particular sin (*cf.* 1 Corinthians 11:30). If the person's sickness comes as the result of some sin, he will no doubt wish to confess and repent of this sin at once. Indeed, his desire for the elders' presence is indicative of his interest in spiritual improvement. Should God grant physical healing and "raise him up," God's healing of the malady (where caused by sin) is evidence that the man's sins have been forgiven as it was the sin which caused the illness.

We'll learn more from James about the power of prayer in the next chapter. For now, remember that whatever else we may say about God's decision to heal, of this we may be certain: God is sovereign and does as He pleases, yet He always does what is right.

What About You?

How would you describe your prayer life? Do you think of prayer as "talking to God?"

Do you sing praise to God regularly in corporate worship? In private worship?

How have verses 14 and 15 been misused by the church?

❊ ❊ ❊

Chapter 23: The Power of a Praying Church
(James 5:16-18)

16 Confess your trespasses to one another, and pray for one another, that you may be healed. The effective, fervent prayer of a righteous man avails much.
17 Elijah was a man with a nature like ours, and he prayed earnestly that it would not rain; and it did not rain on the land for three years and six months.
18 And he prayed again, and the heaven gave rain, and the earth produced its fruit.

I n our day it seems there is no end to the "next big thing" for the church. Media invitations and flashy video promotions promise churches will be "radically changed" by implementing some new program or product. The offers are everywhere and the marketing is slick: "Do you want your church to be powerful and life-changing?" (Who doesn't?!). "Purchase the special 'Gold-Level' package today to bring the most power to your congregation."

But power is not something that can be bought (Acts 8:18-24!). A life-changing church is a church whose members pray. Prayer is the key to a dynamic, influential church.

James teaches about the power of prayer in these verses. Specifically, he teaches about the power of two things: *confession to* one another and *intercession for* one another.

Confession *to* One Another

A biblical church is a church whose members regularly confess to one another. If we ask, "What specifically do they confess to one another?" the answer is—first part of verse 16— "Confess your trespasses to one another"—or as most of the modern translations read, "Confess your sins to one another."

A biblical church is a congregation whose members are in the habit of regularly going to one another and saying something like, "Brother (or sister), I really need to apologize for what I said to you the other day. It was wrong and I was wrong to say it. I'm sorry. Will you forgive me?"

Or, "My sister in Christ, the other day I ignored you when you needed me and it was wrong and I was wrong to do it. I'm sorry. Will you forgive me?"

Or, "Brother, I have harbored some bitterness against you for something I have failed to talk to you about and, rather than talk to *you* about it, I'm afraid I have talked to *others* about it. It was wrong and I was wrong to do it. I'm sorry. Will you forgive me?"

This behavior is consistent with Jesus' teaching in the Sermon on the Mount:

> If you bring your gift to the altar, and there remember that your brother has something against you, leave your gift there before the altar, and go your way. First be reconciled to your brother, and then come and offer your gift (Matthew

5:23-24).

The point is: "Don't attempt to come together for corporate worship when you are harboring ill feelings towards other members of the congregation."

Now think about this with me for just a moment. How many churches are there on any given Sunday whose members are gathering together for worship while harboring feelings of ill will towards one another? Would not this unbiblical behavior be at least one reason why power is lacking? On what basis could we ever expect God to honor a church whose members are not regularly confessing their sins to one another?

"Confess...to *one another*." The assumption is that the offense is against another individual. That individual then, the one with whom we are at odds, is the one to whom we are to go and confess. "Confess your trespasses to one another," not to a priest, not to a pastor, not to a group of friends, and not to anonymous followers on social media. We don't discuss it among co-workers, our neighbors, or even our small group or Sunday school class. "Confess your trespasses to *one another*."

A similar teaching is found in Matthew's Gospel where Jesus provides explicit instruction on those occasions where you believe someone has sinned against you, offending you in some way. What do you do? Do you talk about it to others or do you go to that person directly? Jesus is clear: "If your brother sins against you, go and tell him his fault between you and him alone (Matthew 18:15)."

Indeed Jesus goes on to say what you are to do if the one who has sinned against you "will not hear" you. If your attempts to reconcile with your brother prove unsuccessful, perhaps because he refuses to talk about it or insists he did no wrong, Jesus says, "if he will not hear, take with you one or two more, that 'by the mouth of two or three witnesses every word may be established (Matthew 18:16).'"

Quoting from Deuteronomy 19:15, Jesus instructs believers to bring with them one or two others to talk with the offender—but not before going privately first! This next step occurs only after prior attempts (perhaps several attempts) to address the person individually have failed.

It is important to remember that the hopeful outcome of these attempts to meet with the one who has sinned against you is to "gain" or "win over" your brother, to be reconciled in a demonstration of beautiful, biblical unity.

In the rare occasion of an offending brother refusing to listen to the additional "two or three witnesses," even after (we may suppose) several attempts are made, only then is the matter to be brought before the entire congregation (Matthew 18:17). And even at this point, hope remains for reconciliation, that the individual may "hear the church" and the matter be resolved.

If the still rarer occasion occurs where the individual refuses even to "hear the church," only then is he to be regarded as "a heathen and a tax collector," which is to say, no longer part of the church body.

It is unfortunate where churches err in one of two extremes: either ignoring these corrective measures entirely or, in their zeal to be "a pure church," jump hastily to excommunicating members without taking the necessary intermediary steps, failing to extend to others the same loving forbearance our Lord has shown to us.

The fact that some have abused these biblical principles, however, is no reason to ignore them. A church becomes a powerful church when her members regularly confess their trespasses to one another and refuse to allow sinful behavior to go unchecked.

Remember: we are not to "air our dirty laundry" before others. At the first sign of conflict, we are to go to the individual directly and privately. Additionally, should we ever find ourselves "in the middle" of someone else's problem with another brother, we must "get out of the middle." If a person talks to us, sharing disdain for another brother, we will immediately encourage this individual to follow the biblical teaching, instructing him or her to talk directly to the individual. We help our friend understand how doing so honors the other individual, and we promise our prayers for reconciliation.

Do you know what a firewall is? The first time I learned about a firewall was back in my home church where a construction crew was adding an addition to the main structure of the church building. I noted that every so many feet there was a place where a wall protruded higher than the rest of the roof. It looked kind of funny to me and I couldn't understand why the roof was not flat all the way across. I was told the protrusions in the structure were firewalls. In case a fire broke out in one of those sections, it was unlikely to pass beyond the wall of the next section. More firewalls meant better protection of the integrity of the structure.

James says, "Confess your trespasses to one another," so that the offense in view is treated before it spreads to others. If you have a problem with another person, go to that person directly and talk about it and deal with it right there so that the problem does not spread beyond, doing damage to the rest of the church. Work together with your brother or sister so that the two of you become like a firewall, preventing the fire from spreading to others, protecting the integrity of the congregation.

Confessing our trespasses to one another is closely connected to prayer. Healthy confession *to* one another leads to healthy intercession *for* one another.

Intercession *for* One Another

A biblical church is a church whose members regularly pray for one another. If you have offended me and you come and make it right, I am now in a position not only to forgive you, but now to pray for you—and *vice versa;* if I have offended you and I come and ask for forgiveness, you are now in a position to pray for me.

The image of the firewall again is helpful: here are two people who say, "Let's you and I work this out and pray about it together. Let's be a firewall to make sure this doesn't go beyond us. We will stand together."

And there is further suggestion that our failure to confess to one another and pray for one another may mean that we suffer some kind of sickness as a result, whether emotional, spiritual, or physical. James says at the end of verse 16: "Confess your trespasses to one another, and pray for one another, *that you may be healed.*"

The implication is that a Christian may suffer a sickness of some kind, perhaps *emotional* sickness as a result of harboring ill feelings toward another brother or sister. Or perhaps we are suffering a *spiritual* sickness; we are not growing in our faith or feel distance from God. We may even suffer *physical* sickness because of unconfessed and unforgiven sin.

Beyond question, James' teaching in this verse is powerful. Following his teaching makes for a powerful church. A church whose members pray may be assured of two wonderful truths that will bless their congregation.

God Works *with* Extraordinary Power

James writes, "The effective, fervent prayer of a righteous man avails much." The New Living Translation puts it this way: "The earnest prayer of a righteous person has great power and produces wonderful results."

God works with extraordinary power as He works through the prayers of His people—but note: He works His power through the prayers of "a *righteous* person," a person who endeavors to walk in personal holiness.

Lack of personal integrity, purity, and holiness is one reason why many people find their prayers seemingly unanswered. This teaching is similar to Peter's admonition to husbands in his first epistle: "Husbands...dwell with them [your wives] with understanding, giving honor to the wife...*that your prayers may not be hindered* (1 Peter 3:7)."

We can't expect God to honor our prayers when we are not walking in holiness and righteousness. This does not mean we will be perfect; only Christ is perfect, but it means that we will endeavor daily to walk in righteousness. We will, for example, follow James' teaching about confessing our faults to one another.

If members walk in righteousness, including making certain they are at peace with others in the congregation, and if sin is lovingly confronted and carefully corrected, then they are in a better position for God to work His extraordinary power through them. If it is the prayer of a righteous *person* that "avails much," imagine how much more powerful the church will be when *all* members walk in righteousness!

God Works *through* Ordinary People

It is not unusual for us to exclude ourselves from some of the principles and promises of God. We may assume that only spiritual "superstars" can expect their prayers to "avail much." We may feel inferior, common, or "ordinary."

If so, James' words should encourage us. As an example of an ordinary human being through whom God worked, he brings up the Old Testament prophet Elijah. He says, "Elijah was a man with a nature like ours..." Did you catch that? Elijah was not superhuman. He had "a nature like ours." No different.

But we may protest: "What?! Elijah is *nothing* like us! He's the guy who stood boldly on Mount Carmel and called down fire from heaven in a mighty demonstration of God's miraculous wonder-working power (1 Kings 18: 20-46). He's not at all like me!"

To be sure, it *is* an amazing account of biblical history. Elijah essentially tells wicked King Ahab: "Because you have led the people of Israel into idolatry, God is going to withhold the rains of heaven. You and all the land will experience three and a half years of drought. No rain for three and a half years!"

James reminds us in verse 18 that after the three and a half years of judgment, Elijah prayed and the rain fell. It *is* an incredible story of God's extraordinary power through the prayer of a righteous person. No rain falls until Elijah prays. That's power!

So again, when James describes Elijah as "a man with a nature like ours," or a man just like us, our initial thought may be, "No he is not! He is one-of-a-kind!"

But he really *is* just like us. Elijah's vulnerability, for example, is exposed in the very next chapter (1 Kings 19) where we read of his becoming so despondent that he is near death. King Ahab's wicked wife Queen Jezebel threatened to have Elijah killed by the end of the next day. When Elijah gets word of this, his "mountain top experience" crumbles to a "valley of despair." Fleeing into the wilderness he is so depressed, exhausted, and scared that he prayed that he might die. He says to the Lord, "It is enough! Now, Lord, take my life (1 Kings 19:4)."

Now we see that Elijah is indeed "a man with a nature like ours." Who hasn't experienced the capricious turns from the mountain top to the valley? Most of us are willing to admit to spiritual highs and lows.

Yes, Elijah is just like us. So James means to encourage us. In essence, he says: "Look, undoubtedly God works with extraordinary power. And God delights in working that extraordinary power through *ordinary people*, ordinary people like Elijah and ordinary people like you and me."

What About You?

Is there someone with whom you are at odds? A brother or sister to whom you need to confess your trespasses? What will you do about it this week?

How is your prayer life? If it seems your prayers go unanswered, could it be you are not walking in righteousness?

How do you feel about James' describing Elijah as "a man with a nature like ours?"

❊ ❊ ❊

Chapter 24: Wandering From The Truth
(James 5:19-20)

19 Brethren, if anyone among you wanders from the truth, and someone turns him back,
20 let him know that he who turns a sinner from the error of his way will save a soul from death and cover a multitude of sins.

A friend told me once about a family member named Frank. He would often say, "My name is Frank, and that's what I am." This certainly sounds like James, doesn't it? If there is one thing we have learned about James in these studies it is that he does not mince words. He sugarcoats nothing and gets right to the point. He is frank, direct, straightforward, and real. He is blunt, bold, and candid. His approach, while painful at times, is both real and refreshing.

Consistent with his style throughout, these final two verses of James' letter are succinct, incisively penetrating, and fraught with meaning.

James teaches that Christians are to be involved in the ministry of restoration, bringing back fellow believers who have wandered from the truth, presumably by wandering from the church. Christians are to go after those who have fallen into this error. They must work to turn these erring brothers and sisters back to the truth. Doing so, argues James, is tantamount to the saving of their soul from death and the receiving of God's forgiveness.

There are some straightforward truths for the church here, discernible truths embedded in the text.

It is Possible for a Believer to Wander from the Truth

James supposes the real possibility that someone hearing or reading his letter may "wander from the truth." This wandering is possibly a wandering into heresy, but more likely a wandering away from *living* the truth, falling into sins addressed throughout the letter—sins of being judgmental, sins of the tongue, or sins of worldliness.

It is possible for a believer to wander from the truth. We often sing of this possibility in a well-known hymn:

Prone to wander,
Lord I feel it,
Prone to leave the God I love."[35]

We may ask how this is possible given the fact that Christians have a new nature, are born again, and have the Holy Spirit residing within.

Before we address this question, let us admit that many in the typical church congregation may not be saved. No one knows with absolute certainty who is saved and who is not. When we read the New Testament, it seems the writers never pretend to know that every person to whom they are writing is truly saved.

The New Testament writers write the same way *we* would write if we were writing to our church. We would address the "brethren," not knowing for certain that every brother is in fact a genuine brother. Sadly, there may be some among our gathering who will turn away from the church, turn away from spiritual truth, and walk down a path that leads to hell and destruction. That is simply the reality of the situation.

Recall Jesus' warning: "Not everyone who says to Me, 'Lord, Lord,' shall enter the kingdom of heaven, but he who does the will of My Father in heaven (Matthew 7:21)."

We may address Jesus as "Lord," or refer to Him as "Lord," but that alone is no guarantee we are true believers.

Furthermore, we may perform good deeds and works among the community of faith and not be genuinely saved. Jesus adds:

> Many will say to Me in that day, "Lord, Lord, have we not prophesied in Your name, cast out demons in Your name, and done many wonders in Your name?" And then I will declare to them, "I never knew you; depart from Me, you who practice lawlessness (Matthew 7:22-23)!"

A person can refer to Jesus as "Lord," serve in the church, and perform good deeds among the Christian community, but not be a genuine brother or sister in Christ.

In the Apostle John's first letter he writes of those who left the faith:

> They went out from us, but they were not of us; for if they had been of us, they would have continued with us; but they went out that they might be made manifest, that none of them were of us (1 John 2:19).

James addresses the "brethren" without assuming that every person is, in fact, a brother. This uncertainty notwithstanding, James' truth applies to all: turning a sinner from the error of his way saves his soul from death and covers a multitude of sin.

Having addressed the possibility—if not likelihood—that not

all of James' readers and hearers are genuinely saved, we are comforted knowing that true believers will remain true believers. Authentic Christians will persevere in their faith. They will struggle from time to time, but will finally overcome.

Justification describes the very moment God declares us entirely forgiven of all sin. It happens all at once, at a specific moment in time. But while justification is a precise point in time, sanctification is an ongoing process. Sanctification takes a lifetime. So God changes us, but He does not change us all at once. Much of the change occurs gradually over time, often through the "various trials" mentioned earlier in James' opening chapter.

Because of Christ, Christians are saved, redeemed, and justified forever. Yet, there is still what we often describe as the "sin that remains," the daily struggle with temptation, the daily battle with the "old man" or "the flesh." When we give in to the tug of the world and the flesh, we are at that moment "wandering from the truth."

So it is possible for a Christian to wander from the truth. It is interesting that the original word for "wander" is a word from which we get the word "planet." That's helpful as the term conveys the idea of going off-course, wandering like a planet out of orbit.

This is why it is vitally important for a Christian to endeavor to walk in righteousness every day, reading the Word, communing with God, praying to Him, spending time with God's people, attending worship with other believers, and sharing the gospel with the lost. These actions are the "working out" of the salvation God has "worked within us (Philippians 2:12-13)."

As we endeavor to walk in righteousness, we have the assurance that God is growing us in our sanctification, making us more like Jesus, the One with whom we are assured to spend eternity. As Paul writes to the Corinthians, God "will also confirm you to the end, that you may be blameless in the day of our Lord Jesus Christ (1 Corinthians 1:8; *cf.* Romans 8:30)."

Until that day, however, we battle sin and temptation. James' words remind us that it is possible for a believer to wander from the truth.

It is Assumed another Believer will Turn Him Back

For every person who wanders from the truth, James assumes there will be "someone" who "turns him back." In other words he assumes the church is actively going after those who wander.

Given the immediate context, this work of restoration includes prayer. Christians are to "pray for one another" that they "may be healed (James 5:16)." Certainly the effectual, fervent prayers of many righteous persons increases the likelihood of the restoration of many souls.

In addition to their prayers for a wandering brother, the church will also need to approach the one in error in an effort to "turn him back." James assumes "someone" from the congregation will do this.

This truth calls to mind Jesus' parable of the lost sheep. He supposes a man has a hundred sheep and one of them "wanders" (same word used by James). Jesus asks, "Does he (the man) not leave the ninety-nine and go to the mountains to seek the one that is straying (Matthew 18:12)?" Jesus concludes the parable with this truth: "It is not the will of your Father who is in heaven that one of these little ones should perish (Matthew 18:14)."

James expresses the same concern for the church. He assumes that the church has the same love for wandering members as the man does for wandering sheep—as God does for wandering souls.

Do you love those who have wandered from the truth? Do you

know anyone who has wandered from your Bible study? Your Sunday school class or small group? Your worship services? Have you called to check on them?

Too often we allow fear or pride to overrule the Spirit's promptings to reach out to a wandering brother or sister. You can be sure that Satan wants you to just forget about them or to reason, "They had issues," or, "They were never really connected anyway."

Fear of confrontation or fear of appearing sanctimonious may also impede the work of the Spirit within us. But if we truly love others, we will not allow our fears to keep us from doing what the Bible teaches.

Someone said, "A real friend is someone who always 'gets in your way' when you are 'on your way down.'" Good words!

It is possible for a believer to wander from the truth and it is assumed another believer will turn him back. Thirdly:

It is a Blessing when a Believer is Restored

James teaches that the one who "turns a sinner from the error of his way" will invite a blessing. The blessing is the knowledge that God used him to "save a soul from death and cover a multitude of sins."

When a sinner is turned back, his soul is saved from death—spiritual death—final death, because his sins are "covered." His sins are not covered by the one who turned him back, but by God. Only God can forgive sins. The idea is that God used the caring church member, worked through him to bring about the forgiveness of the wanderer's many sins.

James' teaching raises a few poignant questions: Do you love others enough to go after them when they wander? Do you love them as you love yourself? Are you a real friend—someone who "gets in the way" of another who is "on the way down?"

Since all Christians are to be engaged in the ministry of restoration, let us consider how to live out this truth.

Develop Necessary Character as one Who Restores

If we are to be involved in going after those who have wandered from the truth, there are at least two character qualities that are essential to the work.

Humility

If it is possible for a believer to wander from the truth, then it is possible that one day *we ourselves* may be that very believer. This possibility should give us pause lest we draw boastful conclusions about those who have wandered from the truth.

Recall Jesus' teaching in Matthew's Gospel:

> Why do you look at the speck in your brother's eye, but do not consider the plank in your own eye? Or how can you say to your brother, 'Let me remove the speck from your eye'; and look, a plank is in your own eye? Hypocrite! First remove the plank from your own eye, and then you will see clearly to remove the speck from your brother's eye (Matthew 7:3-5).

Among other things, Jesus teaches that each of us "has issues." We each have some kind of inability to "see clearly." So before we make prejudgments about the errors of another brother or sister, let us humbly remember "the plank" in our own eye.

In the words of the Apostle Paul to the Corinthians: "Let him who thinks he stands take heed lest he fall (1 Corinthians 10:12)." Recall also his teaching on this subject to the churches of Galatia: "Brethren, if a man is overtaken in any trespass, you who are spiritual restore such a one in a spirit of gentleness, considering yourself lest you also be tempted (Galatians 6:1)."

Never become so critical of a struggling Christian, a downcast, seemingly defeated brother or sister in Christ, believing somehow you are "above all that." It could happen to you. Practice humility.

Mercy

Having mercy and showing mercy towards others is essential if we hope to win back those who wander from the truth.

Showing mercy is the primary application of the familiar "Parable of the Good Samaritan." Read it afresh and consider how it may apply to James' teaching:

> And behold, a certain lawyer stood up and tested Him, saying, "Teacher, what shall I do to inherit eternal life?" He said to him, "What is written in the law? What is your reading of it?" So he answered and said, ' "You shall love the Lord your God with all your heart, with all your soul, with all your strength, and with all your mind,' and 'your neighbor as yourself.'" And He said to him, "You have answered rightly; do this and you will live."
>
> But he, wanting to justify himself, said to Jesus, "And who is my neighbor?"
>
> Then Jesus answered and said: "A certain man went down from Jerusalem to Jericho, and fell among thieves, who stripped him of his clothing, wounded him, and departed, leaving him half dead. Now by chance a certain priest came down that road. And when he saw him, he passed by on the other side. Likewise a Levite, when he arrived at the place, came and looked, and passed by on the other side.
> But a certain Samaritan, as he journeyed, came where he was. And when he saw him, he had compassion. So he went to him and bandaged his wounds, pouring on oil and wine; and he set him on his own animal, brought him to an inn, and took care of him.
>
> On the next day, when he departed, he took out two denarii, gave them to the innkeeper, and said to him, 'Take care of

him; and whatever more you spend, when I come again, I will repay you.'

So which of these three do you think was neighbor to him who fell among the thieves?" And he said, **"He who showed mercy on him."**

Then Jesus said to him, "Go and do likewise." (Luke 10:25-37).

Remember: "A real friend is someone who always 'gets in your way' when you are 'on your way down.'"

Develop necessary character as one who restores: humility and mercy. There is something else helpful to us as we apply James' teaching:

Understand the Ultimate Cause of Wandering

Why is it that people wander from the truth, especially in the sense James seems most concerned in his letter: wandering from "living out" the truth?

What happens to individuals that they begin to lose interest in corporate worship, preaching of the Word, small group study, and private devotion? Why exactly do they fall away?

To be sure there are many factors involved in the Christian's going astray. We noted earlier, for example, the Christian's on-going struggle with "the sin that remains," that continual battle with "the flesh" or the "old man." We must not underestimate the need for constant vigilance as we endeavor to walk in holiness.

It is also important to remember that most sin stems ultimately from misplaced desire. A lack of delighting in the all-satisfying Lord Jesus Christ weakens our defenses and awakens our vulnerabilities to wrong desires (much as we discussed in Chapter 4 "Tackling Temptation").

God conveys something of this in the Old Testament through the Prophet Jeremiah: "My people have committed two evils: They have forsaken Me, the fountain of living waters, and hewn themselves cisterns—broken cisterns that can hold no water (Jeremiah 2:13)."

When we forsake the Lord, we stop going to Him in prayer, listening to Him in His Word, and communing with Him in worship both corporately and privately. And when we stop "drinking" from Him, we drink from something else. The prophet says God's people have made their own cisterns or wells, wells he describes as "broken cisterns that can hold no water."

A broken cistern is a container that is cracked, allowing water to slowly seep out while mud slowly seeps in. To drink from a broken cistern is to drink muddy water. Who wants to drink muddy water? A thirsty person will drink from it until he discovers a better, more refreshing and more satisfyingly healthy source.

As persons created in God's image, we often thirst for our Creator without even realizing it. As St. Augustine so famously wrote: "Thou hast formed us for Thyself, and our hearts are restless till they find rest in Thee."[36]

Spiritually we may be drinking muddy water without even realizing it, inadvertently trying to satisfy our spiritual yearnings. It's like trying to quench our thirst with the wrong water, drinking from the wrong well.

When you turn to pornography to make yourself feel better, you are drinking from a broken cistern. When you allow your thoughts to wander into sin and temptation, you are drinking from the wrong well. When you get drunk or use drugs to get high you are substituting living water for muddy water, perhaps without even realizing it.

Jesus said to the woman at the well in John 4:

Whoever drinks of this water will thirst again, but whoever drinks of the water that I shall give him will never thirst. But the water that I shall give him will become in him a fountain of water springing up into everlasting life (John 4:13-14).

We wander from the truth when we forget that Jesus embodies truth (John 14:6). Often unintentionally, we turn to the lies of the Enemy, the one in whom "there is no truth (John 8:44)."

The ultimate cause for wandering from the truth is drinking from the wrong well. Take care to drink from the water of life, the only water that can quench the thirsting of our souls. And do your best to see that others who wander are turned back to the living water of Jesus Christ.

In conclusion, let us read prayerfully the words of an old hymn that speak to the heart of this ministry of restoration:

Though they are slighting Him, still He is waiting,
Waiting the penitent child to receive;

Plead with them earnestly, plead with them gently;
He will forgive if they only believe.

Down in the human heart, crushed by the tempter,
Feelings lie buried that grace can restore;

Touched by a loving heart, wakened by kindness,
Chords that were broken will vibrate once more.

Rescue the perishing, duty demands it;
Strength for thy labor the Lord will provide;

Back to the narrow way patiently win them;
Tell the poor wand'rer a Savior has died.[37]

What About You?

Why are some Christians reluctant to reach out to those who have wandered from the truth?

"If it is possible for a believer to wander from the truth, then it is possible that one day *we ourselves* may be that very believer." Do you agree with this statement? Why or why not?

How do you see your role in the ministry of restoration? Is there someone you need to call or reach out to this week?'

✽ ✽ ✽

Appendix
(Becoming a Christian)

"This is a faithful saying and worthy of all acceptance, that Christ Jesus came into the world to save sinners..." (1 Timothy 1:15)

This verse most succinctly captures the reason the eternal Son of God took on flesh, lived among us for some thirty-three years, died on the cross, and rose from the grave: "to save sinners."

But what does it mean to *be* a sinner? Who *is* a sinner?

In short, a sinner is someone who breaks God's laws; a lawbreaker. A sinner is someone who knows what he ought to do, but he doesn't do it (James 4:17).

Paul writes in Romans 3:23: "all have sinned and fall short of the glory of God." All. Every single person on the planet is a sinner. We have all failed to do consistently and perfectly what the Bible teaches.

If we ever expect to have a relationship with the One True and Living God, then we have to be consistently sinless and perfect all the time. But we aren't. Only God is perfect. He is perfectly holy, perfectly loving, and perfectly just.

We, on the other hand, are *imperfect*. We are unholy. We often act very unjustly. In a word: we are sinners.

And the Bible teaches that "the wages of sin is death" (Romans 6:23). Put another way: "What we get for being sinners is death," spiritual death.

But sin is a *condition* before it is an *action*. We are born sinners. Ephesians 2:1 defines us in our natural state as "dead in trespasses and sins."

We are natural born sinners. So it's not that we first sin and then *become* sinners, but rather that we sin because we *are* sinners. And if nothing changes we remain that way for eternity, separated from God forever in a horrible place called hell, separated because of our sin, unable to stand in God's presence because He is perfect and we are not.

This is what we often call the "bad news" we must first apprehend before we can appreciate the "good news (the meaning of the word gospel)." We cannot fully appreciate what it means to be forgiven until we know that we need forgiveness. All have sinned and fall short of the glory of God.

In order for God to remain just in all His ways, He has to punish our wrongdoing. He can't just forgive our evil acts without punishing us. That would be like an earthly judge simply letting everybody get away with every crime. If you've ever been a victim of a crime and a judge did that, you'd cry, "That's unjust!" And rightly so because the acts of lawbreakers should be punished. Well, we've offended our holy God; we've broken His laws and our sins must be punished.

Here's what makes Christianity so different from every major religion. Every other religion is about earning God's approval: "Do these things and God will accept you. Do this. Do that, and you'll earn a way to God." It's like climbing a ladder of deeds: "Do this, then this, and this, and you'll finally reach God." But it would require an infinite number of rungs or steps to appease an infinite God!

Christianity is not "Do." Christianity is "Done." In other words, Christianity is not about our climbing up a ladder of good deeds to reach God. Christianity is about God's having coming down to us. The eternal Son of God, second Person of the Trinity, comes down to us as in the great Christmas lyric: "Word of the Father now in flesh appearing.[38]"

God enfleshes Himself in human skin and dwells among us for thirty-three years. He lives a perfect life for us. We can't do that, but He can, and He did. He lived without breaking a single law. He can do that because He's God! So He is also able to die as a perfect substitute for our sin, taking our punishment upon Himself. In this way God remains just and justice is served. He has punished sin by punishing *our* sin in *His Son* Jesus Christ.

And on the third day after His death, Christ rises from the dead, demonstrating His power over sin, death, hell, and the grave. He is alive! And if we believe He is the rightful King of our lives, we can be saved from the penalty of our sin and have eternal life in Him.

Indeed, when we place our faith in Jesus Christ, all of our sin is imputed--or charged--to Christ and Christ's perfect record of obedience is credited to us (2 Corinthians 5:21)!

Have you received Christ as Lord and Savior? If not, will you now receive Him, trusting Him alone for forgiveness of sin? The Bible says He is the only way for you to be forgiven of sin and to enter into a saving relationship with God (John 14:6).

Admit your need. Admit you are a sinner in need of God's forgiveness.

Turn from trusting in anything or anyone else and trust only in Jesus Christ.

Believe that Jesus Christ lived a perfect life for you, died for your sins on the cross, rose from the grave, and is your only way to acceptance with God.

If you are ready to take this step, talk to God in prayer. Share with Him your understanding of what He has done for you and how you are willing to turn from your sin in repentance and trust Him as your Savior and Lord. The following prayer may be a helpful guide as you talk to God and share the desire of your heart:

> Lord Jesus Christ, thank you for making it possible for me to have peace with God! I believe that when You died You were paying the penalty for my sins. I admit that I am weaker and more sinful than I ever before believed, but through You I understand I am more loved and accepted than I ever dared hope. I thank You for paying my debt, bearing my punishment, and offering forgiveness. I turn from my sin and receive You as Savior. Thank you for the gift of eternal life!

If you are receiving Jesus Christ as Lord and Savior, I would love to hear from you! Contact me at https://preachingtruth.org/contact and share your decision to trust Jesus. I will pray for you and help you get connected to a local church.

Endnotes

[1]   *Antiquities of the Jews* , Book 20, chap. 9, sec. 1

[2]   *Ecclesiastical History*, 1995, pp. 75-76

[3]   *Memoirs*, Book V.

[4]   Available as a pdf from https://www.desiringgod.org/books/dont-waste-your-cancer accessed May 18, 2020.

[5]   Chapter 12, "Communicable Attributes of God" in *Systematic Theology*, 194.

[6]   Interestingly, the original Greek word translated "tempted" may also be translated "trial." The sense is best determined by context. If God is immediately behind the action, the word should be translated "trial." If Satan is immediately behind the action, the word is best translated "temptation." When God tests, it is for good; our good and His glory. When Satan tempts, it is always for bad; bringing about evil.

[7]   *31 Days of Purity*, ed., Tim Challies; www.challies.com/articles/31-days-of-purity-the-joy-of-salvation; accessed May 20, 2020

[8]   I am indebted to David Roper for the essence of this illustration though he utilizes it differently in his helpful book on James: *Growing Slowly Wise: Building a Faith that Works* (Grand Rapids: Discovery House, 2000), 56-57.

[9]   Commentary on James 2. "William Barclay's Daily Study Bible" https://www.studylight.org/commentaries/dsb/james-2.html 1956-1959 (accessed May 21, 2020).

[10]   *Ibid.*

[11]   Paraphrase of John Calvin, *Antidote to the Council of Trent* (1547), responding to Canon 11 of the sixth session.

[12]   Edwards was an 18th Century pastor who preached in America in the mid-1700s. He was also the founding president of what is now Princeton University.

[13]   Available at http://www.biblebb.com/files/edwards/truegrace.htm accessed July 11, 2017

[14]   Grudem, Wayne. *Systematic Theology* (page 1145).

[15]   *The Works of John Newton, Volume I.*

[16]   *Reformation & Revival* Vol.9, Winter 2000, 19)."

[17]   "10-Year-Old With Matches Started a California Wildfire," *The New York Times,* November 1, 2007.

[18]   "The Power of the Tongue," available at https://www.danielakin.com/the-power-of-the-tongue/ accessed May 24, 2020.

[19]   Source unknown.

[20]   I cannot recall the source of this quote, but I believe I heard it on a recorded sermon of one of Prime's students.

[21]   *cf.* ESV and NIV.

[22]   Barclay, William. *Daily Study Bible, Chapter 4,* available at https://www.studylight.org/commentaries/dsb/james-4.html accessed May 25, 2020.

[23]   "A Wartime Bomb, Unearthed in Germany, Recalls Darker Days," available at: https://www.nytimes.com/2015/05/28/world/europe/decades-later-germans-still-dread-the-bombs-that-didnt-go-off.html accessed May 25, 2020.

[24]   I believe this to be the proper translation rather than the capital "S" of the NKJV. At the same time, the text could refer to the Holy Spirit in the following rendering: "The Spirit who dwells in us opposes our jealousy."

[25]   Alec Motyer, *The Message of James: The Bible Speaks Today* (Downers Grove: IVP, 1985), 157.

[26]   G.F. Barbour, *The Life of Alexander Whyte*, D.D., Hodder & Stoughton; Seventh Edition edition (1925), 316.

[27]   Chapman, J. Wilbur. "One Day," *ca.* 1908, Public Domain

[28]   Ryle, J.C., *Expository thoughts on the Gospels, with the text complete, Volume 1* (London: William Hunt and Company), 352.

[29]   Piper, John, "I Seek Not What is Yours, but You" available from www.desiringgod.org/messages/i-seek-not-what-is-yours-but-you, accessed May 27, 2020.

[30]   Alcorn, Randy. *The Treasure Principle* (Colorado Springs: Multnomah, 2001), 73.

[31]   Henry, Matthew. *James - Commentary On The Whole Bible: Volume VI-III-Titus - Revelation* ed. by Anthony Uyl (Woodstock, Ontario: Devoted Publishing), 140.

[32]   I am indebted to Tim Keller for this phrase "Your hand is always on the Bible," heard in his sermon, "Communication" available at https://gospelinlife.com/downloads/communication-5831/ accessed May 28, 2020.

[33]   Scriven, Joseph. "What A Friend We Have In Jesus." 1855, Public Domain

[34]   Robertson, A.T., *Word Pictures in the New Testament*; James 5 available https://www.studylight.org/commentaries/rwp/james-5.html at accessed May 28, 2020.

[35]   Robinson, Robert. "Come Thou Fount of Every Blessing." 1758, Public Domain

[36]   *Confessions*, Book I, Chapter 1.

[37]   Crosby, Frances J. "Rescue the Perishing." 1869, Public Domain

[38]   Wade, John Frances. "O Come, All Ye Faithful," 1751, Public Domain

Afterword

Before you go--we would love to hear your feedback about *You're Either Walking The Walk Or Just Running Your Mouth!*

If you found this book useful, we would be grateful for your short review on Amazon. Your support makes a difference as every review is read personally.

If you'd like to leave a review, find a link to the book at https://amazon.com/author/toddlinn

Also, sign up for future book release information and promotions here: https://preachingtruth.org/book-release-sign-up

Thanks for your support!

* * *

About The Author

Todd A. Linn

Todd earned his PhD in preaching from The Southern Baptist Theological Seminary in 2004.

With 23 years of pastoral ministry, Todd identifies as a preacher, teacher, writer, and coffee drinker. His thoughts and resources can be found at preachingtruth.org.

Made in the USA
Monee, IL
04 August 2020

37576142R00138